D0629460

THE TOTAL IMAGE

OR
SELLING JESUS
IN THE
MODERN AGE

Virginia Stem Owens

GRAND RAPIDS
WILLIAM B. EERDMANS PUBLISHING COMPANY

Library of Congress Cataloging in Publication Data

Owens, Virginia.
  The total image.

  1. Mass media in religion—United States.
2. Christianity and culture. I. Title.
BV652.95.A3   269'.2   80-11278
ISBN 0-8028-1833-1

CONTENTS

Chapter I:

THE RADIO AND
THE PSALMS

". . . he believed if a man were permitted to make all the ballads, he need not care who should make the laws of a nation."—Andrew Fletcher of Saltoun

BEING AN HABITUAL SORT OF CREATURE, I get up every weekday, relishing a few quiet minutes of morning in solitude before the rest of my household begins to stir. Then routinely I turn a black knob that instantaneously admits an unremitting stream of late twentieth-century American culture into a home we consider Christian. Scores from last night's baseball game. Ads for automobiles. Traffic reports from a helicopter. An ad for condominiums. Weather forecasts. An ad for a headache remedy. And finally the hard news. Floods, airplane crashes, terrorists, bizarre murders, and unidentified epidemics.

By the time the coffee has perked and the toast has browned, the world that Wordsworth complains is too much with us hangs like discolored haze over the sliced oranges and the honey pitcher. And when the black knob is flicked off for the morning psalm reading around the breakfast table, effectually damming up the torrent of word-carried American culture, what happens to that cloud still hanging over our heads? How does it affect us?

One answer is that this rather ordinary family cannot effectively lift up its heart under such a load of cacophony heralding human folly and suffering. I have not found this to be altogether true, however. In fact, the very nonchalance of the knob-turning, the infinitesimal amount of energy the act entails, testifies to the ease with which the weight is shrugged off. We are just as jolly as ever as we entreat God to confound our enemies or bid the trees of the field to clap their hands and the hills to leap for joy.

1

The second answer is that the radio's outpouring should be an ever-present reproach, reminding us of our duty to do something about prison reform, rapid transit, and better health care. It implies that cavorting hills and clapping trees don't have much relevance to the shortage of fossil fuel. Once again, I find this answer does not fit the reality. We are unabashed by its reproach. The vision of a world where trees tremble in delight and hills jump for joy is more exciting to all of us than one where rapid transit trains run on time and nuclear energy.

No. Frustrating as it is to try to balance the radio and the psalms at the breakfast table, I suspect we will go on living with both. Being in but not of the world has always been the central Christian dilemma and one that, I am pleased to point out, has produced a welter of creative answers. It brought forth the Desert Fathers, the great structures of monasticism, the initial impetus of the Reformation, the missionary orders of the Renaissance, and John Wesley. It is even responsible for the permanent settlement of North America by Europeans. When Christians have found the weight of their culture insupportable, they have discovered, even in frustration and withdrawal, ways to leaven it.

Undeniably there have also emerged inadequate and harmful responses to cultural frustration. Going all the way back to the Gnostics, possibly the first Christian heretics, we find folk for whom the world was indeed too much. And let us not be overly quick to feel our superiority to these world-deniers. Dirt, filth, disease, hunger, death, brutality such as we have never known engulfed the ancient world. Who would not have been tempted to deny this sort of world simply to retain one's sanity? There were certainly none of the avenues that we have today for alleviating social deficiencies. No public health clinics, no free public education, no Food and Drug Administration, no prison reform. In short, no *earthly* hope of lessening the harshness of ordinary life.

The early church was hard pressed to relieve the physical suffering of even its own members, much less devise the sorts of grandiose plans we make nowadays for combating hunger and pain globally. So it was a perfectly reasonable response on the part of the Gnostics to protect themselves by denying the physical world.

Hard upon their heels followed a more exotic and shorter-lived group, the Circumcellions, mentioned here as an example of the bizarre forms of cultural frustration. The Circumcellions, who flourished during the lifetime of Augustine, were Christian kamikaze squads, bent on winning a martyr's way out of the world. When the state refused to oblige them, they would fall upon bewildered travellers in lonely places and demand that they dispatch them into a better world. Those who refused to perform this service were themselves threatened with death.

The Reformation itself, out of which came a totally new tradition for a new age, providing badly needed innovations in the way Christians were to live in the world, also produced some shameful false starts and aborted efforts. The peasantry of northern Europe, for example, led to believe that freedom from oppression by the church and its unscrupulous representatives went hand in hand with freedom from other sources of economic oppression, were brutally suppressed by fearful Christian princes. The years that saw Christian set against Christian in violence, each walled city at war with its neighbor, provided a poor paradigm for a response to the world.

Nor was the settlement of North America by religious dissenters an unadulterated success. When these transplanted European Christians were confronted with an alien culture their response was more often exploitation and arrogance than the sensitive and responsible evangel-spreading by men like Roger Williams and John Eliot.

Although American religious history never produced anything quite so dramatic as the Circumcellions, bizarre sects spawned freely in the atmosphere of religious toleration. Almost invariably based on some special revelation to a charismatic personality, they had at their core some form of cultural revolution. When Mother Ann Lee, founder of the Shakers, insisted not simply on communism but also celibacy, she was cross-pollinating the ancient gnosticism with the new economic orders. The result, however, was sterility: the Shakers have gone the way of the dinosaurs.

When Joseph Smith came up with a different mixture of social and economic structures—polygamy and pragmatism—he too was making a cultural revolution. The result was a fecundity that is thriving even yet in the soil of American culture. The Mormon church owns controlling interest in soft drink empires, oil companies, television shows, and the state of Utah. What could be more American?

If the Christian response to its surrounding environment has historically been either withdrawal or reformation, it is this very practical sort of stance toward the world that is the basis for a third option today. A growing number of Christians is shrewdly settling into an accommodation of American culture. This shift has been so slick, so smooth that we are only haunted by some nebulous discomfort, some unarticulated feeling that something somewhere is not quite right. We squirm over a supposedly religious bumper sticker or switch off a television program in disgruntlement. Then we feel guilty and take ourselves to task for judging the motives of others who are obviously sincere in their efforts to evangelize. After all, who are we to quibble over mere bad taste? At least they're doing something, aren't they?

Doing something, anything, has become an established American virtue. Action, in and of itself, is unquestioned. In public education, for example, it is now a truism that we learn by doing. The notion that learning is essentially passive is pedagogical heresy. The student must "participate" in the "process" of learning. "Do something!" is the great corporate cry sent up to politicians, teachers, economists, scientists, doctors. And the church.

What the church does best—preach, worship, and partake of the sacraments—is, however, discounted as ineffectual ritual and not "real" action. Should the church refuse to be cast in the role of hustler, then the para-ecclesiastical storm troopers stream in to bridge the gap. Media blitzes, advertising campaigns, concert circuits, radio and television networks, clubs, camps, conferences. All aspects of American culture are duplicated and supposedly baptized. One feels securely a part of the mainstream.

This practical sort of cultural accommodation is not to be confused with those periods of human history when cultures were homogeneous. Then, whether Christian or pagan, the values and spirit of a community were shared by all its participants. The Christian culturizers of today, however, certainly deny that they support the values of the secular society in which they find themselves. But at the same time they are eager to adopt the methods and style of that very society they deplore.

Yet has anyone analyzed and evaluated with any clarity this aping of secular culture? Are we so caught up with the American ideal of action that we have neglected to question the means by which the action is accomplished? Are we so enthralled by the sight of superstars endorsing Jesus on TV that we shrug off the trivializing effect of the deodorant ads it is sandwiched between?

Asking these sorts of questions is so foreign to the pragmatic mind that they seem at best annoying and at worst impertinent and ungrateful. The only question admitted as valid by a pragmatist is "does it work?" Yet never before have we so desperately needed some guide, some scale of judgment for determining, on grounds other than pragmatism, what is fitting and proper, in the original sense of that word, to an expression of the Christian faith. For at least the past few decades all the forms of our expression have been borrowed, even stolen, from our surrounding milieu, and that very uncritically. The results have been ridiculous, absurd, and sometimes heretical.

We have not been without warning on this score. Marshall McLuhan's maxim—the medium is the message—has by this time penetrated to every corner of our literate population. But somehow Christians seem to have missed the connection. We are still awkwardly juggling the three options: (A) shut out or withdraw from the world, the traditional but increasingly unpopular conservative point of view; (B) change the world, still clung to by disheartened liberals; or the new entry (C), beat them at their own game. Option

C is gaining support among mavericks from both A and B who are impatient with their own lack of results. Of course A and B don't yet recognize that they have united under a common flag of cultural accommodation. They still think that their squabbles over points of politics and theology are more significant than their mutual eagerness to participate in communal technology. Actually, they have assumed a common stance toward the world while using different reasons to justify it. The conservatives say, "If the devil can use these means to seduce men's souls, why can't we use them for his salvation?" The question to them is rhetorical. The liberals, somewhat more pompously, say, "God can work through any aspect of human society to bring about his will." Yet they are both talking about the same issue, say the buying and selling of names of computer data banks for mailing lists. The two apologists would perceive the issue as political since one would be buying the list to mail anti-World Council of Churches brochures while the other would be selling his list to subsidize an anti-Rhodesian task force.

Unfortunately, our perception of our situation has become so thoroughly politicized—a feat produced by technology—that the importance of other aspects of human life has been stunted. The space we allow in our consciousness for essential and unchanging human activity has shrivelled to insignificance. The problem of the radio and the psalms is not, as has been so long and fruitlessly assumed, one of politics. Yet politics has become the convenient dumping ground for all theological problems. Unless we have submitted all conflicts to the political litmus test, we believe we cannot begin to evaluate positions. For example, I have never heard H. Richard Niebuhr's book *Christ and Culture* discussed in any other than political terms. Although the book itself is concerned with a much broader understanding of culture, of which politics is only a subcategory, those who use it as a base for explaining their way of relating to the world do so only in political terms. They never use it as apologetics for the movies they see or the clothes they wear.

Even such publications as *Sojourners*, a magazine of

the evangelical left, which sees its calling to be a critic of the prevailing culture, interprets that calling in almost purely political terms. Although it has taken upon itself the "rebuilding of the church," almost every word of its copy addresses the government, not the church, nor any other aspect of human culture. Unfortunately, they too have fallen victim to what Jacques Ellul has called *The Political Illusion.*

> What we see here is the result of the process of politicization in our selves: the penetration into our unconscious of the "truth" that an ultimately political process rules our lives. As a result we are led to render all questions political. Those which are not must then be politicized because our frame of mind dictates that ultimately everything is political. (p. 15)

This much must be said for both Mormons and the new Christian culturizers. At least they recognize that there is more to human life than politics. When the dietary laws of the Mormon church forbid the use of coffee, tea, or other such stimulants, the impact on the daily lives of Mormons is much greater than all the politically couched appeals of the Christian church to eat less meat for the good of grain-needy neighbors. In fact, it is ironic that the obligatory Friday meat fasts of the Roman Catholic Church probably accomplished more in that direction than all the subsequent hunger campaigns, even though such fasts were undertaken purely for the spiritual good of its people and with none of the admonishing statistical charts pointing out how much of this world's goods Americans consume. Indeed, why is it that such statistics are always broken down into political units? Wouldn't it be more instructive to the church to know how much Christians as a group consume? Are Methodists greater carnivores than Mennonites? Do Baptists eat higher on the hog than Presbyterians?

The church, disastrously, has discounted almost every form of human endeavor other than what can be politicized. "In other eras," says Ellul,

> a man could be regarded as being committed by being involved in the structure and the collective life of his society—in arts, science, religion, etc. He is no longer considered 'committed', however, unless the implications of his activity are directly

political. To participate in non-political activities that are
nevertheless definitely related to our society is regarded as
without value. A poet restricting himself to being a poet without signing petitions or manifestos would immediately be ac-
cused of retiring to his ivory tower.

Actually we find that the tests most often used to evaluate cultures dead and gone are not political but aesthetic.
We marvel, for example, at the cathedral builders and tap-
estry workers of medieval Europe, searching these artifacts
for signs of faith and value. The political machinations of
the Electors and princes we find either tiresome or ludi-
crous. They tell us nothing about what man was made for.
It is the picture of the unicorn approaching the outstretched
hand of the Virgin, spanning centuries, that still has inexplicable power over our own imaginations, even though our
culture no longer believes in either unicorns or virginity.
Our best clue to understanding ancient cultures has
always been their artifacts. If we wonder what it is in human psychology that allowed for the notion of god-kings in
ancient Egypt and Rome, we are most illumined by the pyramids and coliseum, the Sphinx and the Colossus of Rhodes.
Tutankhamen was a political nonentity in Egypt's dynastic
line, hardly a heartbeat in the rigid rhythm of the realm.
But the treasures of his tomb evoke unaccountable responses in us still. The masks, the jewelry, the small effigies
tell us of a death-defying desire to penetrate eternity, the
imagination shaping the otherwise inarticulate longings of
the spirit. Whatever conjectures about prehistoric man we
may amuse ourselves with quarreling over, the only thing
we empirically know about him, as G. K. Chesterton has
pointed out in *The Everlasting Man*, is that he drew pictures. Not just crude stick figures we can dismiss as childish
and primitive, but scenes of surpassing grace and purity.
Pictures to make us ponder the fact that, of all human en-
deavors, there is no "progress" in art.
Yet when we evaluate current culture, the notion that
life is made up of problems and solutions, most of which are
political, pervades our common consciousness. No one is
asking questions about the signs of faith we will leave be-

hind when this age departs. Perhaps politics is a way of distracting ourselves from confronting the depleted Christian imagination of our day. We have no Mozarts or Bachs, no catacombs or cathedrals, no Dantes or Donnes.

What has happened to the Christian imagination? Why is it so sickly and second-rate? Have we become genetically inferior to the rest of society? Has the promise that the old will dream dreams and the young see visions been revoked for us? If secular society offers only Freudian dreams and drug-induced visions, are we really offering anything better to the world of the spirit or the senses?

These are difficult questions. They make us feel defensive. Our first response is to point out that the secular imagination is not producing very nourishing works of the spirit either. Or we simply shrug off as insignificant such insubstantial and unmarketable products as dreams, visions, and the imagination. In short, we acquiesce, by one rationalization or another, to the captivity of the Christian imagination, betraying our willingness to leave it locked away and despairing of deliverance.

Perhaps more direct and even harder questions are necessary.

Will archaeologists in the future be able to distinguish between a church building and a savings and loan edifice?

Will our music, saved for posterity on undecaying vinyl discs and strips of magnetic tape, be distinguished or distinguishable in any way from its secular counterpart?

Will the labors of future scholars make it possible to sort out the tatters of bumper stickers advertising Jesus into a significantly distinct category from those proclaiming Disneyland and the Dallas Cowboys?

Why are Christian TV personalities dressed and coiffured to duplicate almost exactly their secular counterparts? What *is* a "TV personality"?

Why are mainline denominations struggling to develop task forces, departments, committees, and programs to get a foot in the magic door of mass media? Are such structures themselves the actual and unwitting products of the shrivelled faculty of the imagination of the late twentieth-century church; the best creative response our spirits can now manage to the gospel?

What sign of Christ will be left behind when this age departs? Perhaps the answer lies in another question. Do we believe that it *will* depart? Have even Christians been seduced by the secular faith that our technology is unassailable by either outrageous fortune or the justice of God? Do we instead see ourselves moving down the corridor of the future in a scenario created by Stanley Kubrick and Captain Kirk of the *Enterprise*? Are our promised dreams and visions being mediated by technological triumphalism?

When we ask these questions about creativity and the imagination, we are not concerned simply with the individual production of "art objects." The crisis of Christian aesthetics is not assuaged by displays in the lobby of "liturgical art." The question involves our whole culture, huge populations, this present age. An individual artist—Christian, pagan, or atheist—always works in response to his cultural environment, sometimes in violent reaction, sometimes with strong support. Human creations never take place in a sterile vacuum but in an atmosphere heavy with the germs of culture, the shared perceptions of an age. Although the work of an artist may be solitary, it represents the possibilities available to humanity at that particular time and place.

This book is meant to be both a confession and a call. First of all a confession that at best we Christians are currently poor imitators of the cultural productions of our society. We have so given ourselves to that central value of a technological society—efficiency—that we have neglected every other value in our mad rush toward some supernal Nielsen rating. Results, here and now and verifiable by marketing research, have become our sole criteria for judging any creation by a Christian body. We have forgotten the comparison Jesus made of the kingdom of God to a man scattering seed which "sprout and grow, he knows not how."

Not surprisingly our results are as shoddy as the society's they imitate. Our imagination—open to redemption and transformation by that word of power that upholds the universe—has failed our times. We are frightened, incompetent stewards who are starving the people. Where the spirit needs nourishing by dreams and visions, we are substituting the junk food of media hype, convinced that if such tactics can sell detergent they can also sell Jesus.

Second, this is a call—not a solution, not a blueprint for an arts program of the church, but a summons to free the captive vision of Christ's people from the constricting notion that what we are involved in is a giant advertising campaign for salvation. Advertising, no matter how good the market analysis, is not "the fruit that remains" that we are appointed to bear in the Gospel of John. John's written witness is itself that kind of fruit. It is among other things a creation of image-evoking words that have penetrated every culture it has ever touched. John's "lamb of God," his "light that shines in darkness," the image of the Good Shepherd is the stuff of which our common understanding of reality is made. Even the secular world has for centuries relied on this picture of what is valuable in human existence. Yet it was a very low-budget undertaking. This despite the recent claim by Pat Robertson, president of the Christian Continental Broadcasting Network, that the church will never be able to do much as long as it is poor and underfinanced. "The billion dollar category is what is needed to be truly effective," he says (*Your Church*, May/June, 1979, p. 15).

We can't go back to building cathedrals. Dante's *Divine Comedy* has already been written. It is as useless to try to duplicate the treasures of the past as it is to imitate the productions of the present. The creative powers of those made in the image of Creator, however, can be, even as Lazarus, called forth from the grave. The shape these powers may take is still unknown to us, but that is no reason to retreat to the molds provided by a society insufficient to succor the spirit. It requires courage to rise from the dead. First of all it is going to be a difficult exploration, digging around in the rubble. For one thing it is hard to separate words we hold holy from forms we find inhuman. Anything the name of Jesus is attached to we are reluctant to tamper with. But we will never free the captive creativity of Christianity as long as we insist on enslavement—and finally entombment—with the false aesthetics of our time.

Chapter II:

ON AND OFF CAMERA: MEDIA AS METAPHYSICAL METAPHOR

"He was part of my dream, of course—but then I was part of his dream, too!"—Alice Through the Looking Glass

ITTING IN A DARKENED movie theater, reflected light flickering across my eleven-year-old face, I watched Ann Blyth's black curls blowing back from her alabaster profile as she stood at the prow of the reformed pirate captain's ship, smiling serenely at the ultimate significance she sailed towards. The music swelled in rhythm with the waves as the camera pulled away, reducing her to an upright, windblown silhouette in the middle of a cobalt sea. The music crashes to a close. "The End" appears superfluously across the screen in antique typeface. The stricture loosens slowly in my throat and I stumble out into the startling afternoon sunlight. I feel I am somehow leaving life behind me in the dark at the matinee—all its poignancy, its great events, its significant moments—and retreating reluctantly into a mundane, makeshift world, colored and tasting like cardboard. I consecrate myself, unconsciously, to reshaping reality into a semblance of life on the screen.

I did not know of Plato then, nor his belief that what we see around us are mere images flickering on a cave wall while outside a reality of substance waits to be discovered. In fact, I had in a sense reversed his metaphor. I took the flickering film for a more substantial reality than the sidewalk and glare outside.

Susan Sontag, a caustic critic of American culture, began her book *Styles of Radical Will* with a solid brass tack of the sort we are always promising to get down to. "Every era," she claims, "has to reinvent the project of 'spirituality' for itself. (Spirituality = plans, terminologies, ideas of de-

13

portment aimed at resolving the painful structural contradictions inherent in the human situation, at the completion of human consciousness, at transcendence.)"

Perhaps Sontag's notion of inventing, or reinventing, spirituality is too purposeful. Certainly when Edward Muybridge invented the first motion picture in 1889 by a series of still photographs of the feet of a galloping horse, he was not consciously constructing a new form of spirituality in order to resolve the painful contradictions of the human situation. In fact, he only thought up the clever device in order to win a bet. He wanted to prove that all four of the horse's hooves were off the ground at the same time. Nevertheless, because of Edward Muybridge's invention my young head was swimming with ideas of deportment that I believed would complete my own human consciousness and make it possible to transcend the cardboard reality on which I was starving.

I dreamed movies. Not strange, blurred, surrealistic ordinary dreams, but complete, full-length features. I put myself to sleep every night by reinventing films wherein I played various heroines. Myself as Jane Russell, Katherine Hepburn, Deborah Kerr.

I have ever since, at first unconsciously and later with growing awareness, continued to "view" life as a movie. Or at least to hope that it somehow achieved the heightened reality of a movie. Some moments, inevitably, have to be lived "off camera": brushing one's teeth, taking out the garbage, changing diapers. Even after *cinema verité* came along with its discovery of a gold mine of heretofore unfilmed scenarios and the elevation of the ordinary, I never saw a shot of any of those three rather common human activities. It took television to discover them. But more of that later.

In contradistinction to the inevitable off-camera moments are those spent on camera. Adolescence particularly seemed to be a time when the camera rolled incessantly. There was the nobody-understands-me scene when the camera silently followed me into my bedroom where I flounced on the bed in bitter tears, burying my head in the pillow. And the triumphal scene in which I sailed past a line of envious detractors to receive my National Honor Society pin. Of course, cheerleader would have been a better role, but then one didn't have much control over the casting. And the big kiss scene. I often wonder what teenage sex life was like before the age of movies.

Even when nothing particularly film-worthy happened, there were always reruns or rushes to whirl through my head. Projecting the future had a very literal sense for me. It meant setting up scenarios in my mind—my career girl apartment in a big city, my marriage to an oil tycoon, my deathbed speech, delivered in a whisper but amplified by a boom microphone, after contracting a fatal disease in an African field station hospital.

My family kept telling me to stop dramatizing myself. What they didn't realize was that to stop dramatizing would have been to stop living, to surrender spirituality. The hidden camera was always there, waiting to record the significant moment. A moment when there was a pause, a turn, a glance, and the music rose in the background.

As I got older, my world tended to slip more and more into Book instead of Movie. None of the above scenarios developed. I went to college, got married, had two babies. Not the sort of stuff movies are made of. But Jane Austen built a tidy monument to herself out of such domestic material. There is, of course, no rising music piped into the background of books. You have to create it yourself, just as you create the pictures the words evoke. I can testify to the fact that it takes an unimaginable amount of energy to translate one's life into a book when it consists largely of baby food and broken washing machines.

But the techniques I had learned with movies—the projections, the editing, the sorting out of significant scenes— stood me in good stead during this Book period. Interiors, important to Jane Austen, took on new meaning to me. Kitchen curtains could be an outward and visible sign of the inner state of one's consciousness. Clothes were a statement to the world of one's spiritual situation. Even though the materials seemed more meager, like the decision of whether to have chili or chicken divan when company came for dinner on Friday night, shaping them into a book took considerably more skill and effort than movie-life where the costumes and props came ready-made from Twentieth Century Fox. There was a lot one could do, however, with interior dialogues, nuances of meaning, and stream-of-consciousness that was impossible with movie-imagination. Still, Jane Austen always bore an astounding resemblance to Ann Blyth when she appeared in the spotlight of my mind.

However, by the time my children were getting out of diapers and I was going back to graduate school, movie-life was waning in America. The old movie cult was dying; Ann Blyth had degenerated into Doris Day. The vast imagination machine, hidden away inside special temples with heavily evocative names such as The Palace, Monaco, Aladdin, and Bijou, was replaced in American culture by infinite tiny versions of itself—alike but importantly different. In America one no longer had to pay a visit to the big temple to receive spiritual satisfaction. Like the Roman hearth gods, there was at least one television set in every home.

Gods have always had a tendency to vie amongst themselves for the loyalty of the populace. Now Diana, now Apollo, now Mithras held the upper hand in the ancient Mediterranean world. And Thor and Odin were driven into Iceland by determined Norwegian monks. All gods, it seems, are jealous.

What accounted for this shift in allegiance from movies to television as the temples of American spirituality? Novelty, economics, ease of access? Certainly these were factors, just as trade routes and military victories were factors in the ascendancy or decline of the various deities in the near east. But before we wholly demythologize either Diana or TV, let us in fairness admit that both made certain claims on the human imagination that could be met by no other mechanism currently available.

I cannot speak for the female huntress who ran her victims to ground with her pack of hounds, but of television in the early sixties I, like every other American, have some direct experience. The appeal of this miniature movie box was not in the way it imitated movies but in its added dimension—instant real movie-life. It did not have to depend on fictional stories which might or might not be capable of suspending disbelief. I, for example, had given up all hope by that point of capture by a pirate. But the possibilities of real life itself being dramatized into world-shaking significance was the new dimension television offered. A new and more photogenic President was on the scene. A cast of thousands assembled in public squares. The news was the vehicle by which this amazing possibility presented itself. And what made news in the sixties was assassinations.

The two components buttressed one another. Just as the assassinations would perhaps never have occurred without the promise of appearing on television, so television would never have become the final arbiter of American politics without the assassinations.

Walker Percy's fictional Lancelot articulates the compulsion of this new spirituality for all of us:

> News! Christ, what is so important about the news? Ah, I remember. We were wondering who was going to get assassinated next. Sure enough, the next one did get killed. There it was, the sweet horrid dread we had been waiting for. It was the late sixties and by then you had got used to a certain rhythm of violence so that one came home with the dread and secret expectation that the pace had quickened, so that when the final act was done, the killing, the news flash: the death watch, the funeral, the killing during the funeral, one watched as one watches a lewd act come to climax, dry-mouthed, lips parted, eyes unblinking and slightly bulging—and even had the sense in oneself of lewdness placated. (*Lancelot*, Farrar, Straus & Giroux, 1977, p. 72)

Some may believe that Walker Percy has overstated the case. Remember, however, that he is writing a book, a medium that presently requires some exaggeration merely to keep in the ring with other forms of communication.

McLuhan notes the peculiar interplay of the televising process in the actual murder of Oswald:

Jack Ruby shot Lee Oswald while tightly surrounded by guards who were paralyzed by television cameras. The fascinating and involving power of television scarcely needed this additional proof of its peculiar operation upon human perceptions. The Kennedy assassination gave people an immediate sense of the television power to create depth involvement, on the one hand, and a numbing effect as deep as grief, itself, on the other hand. . . . The banal and ritual remark of the conventionally literate, that TV presents an experience for passive viewers, is wide of the mark. . . . The guards who failed to protect Oswald were not passive. They were so involved by the mere sight of the TV cameras that they lost their sense of their merely practical and specialist task. (*Understanding Media*, New American Library, 1966, pp. 292-293)

In other words, the guards were more immersed in TV-life, as we all were during those days of continuous telecasting, than they were in "real" life which had become disastrously inconsequential.

Like a Greek chorus, rioters took to the streets to add their comments to this juggernaut of national tragedy, a glib but curiously apt name for what was happening in America. For like the Sophoclean cycle, one horrific event fed into another with slow-moving inevitability. Assassinations into riot into Vietnam into Watergate. All of it televised. Instantaneously. The dream promised by the old fifties television series "You Are There" had ultimately come to fruition. The continual telecasting of the Watergate hearings involved fully as many viewers in what they hoped would be catharsis as did the first act Kennedy funeral.

Pushed to its final extremity, this involvement in TV-life had implications that could have been healthily comic had proper attention been paid them. For example, some of my relatives in East Texas, most of whose information about the outside world is mediated by television, were convinced that the 1969 moon shot was not real but rather a television mock-up. Their inflated faith in television to accomplish anything and their deflated sense of meaningful activity in the "real" world had led to an Alice-in-Wonderland state where all categories were turned topsy-turvy. Do not dismiss them as merely ignorant and provincial. In the seventies we had a movie made on this same supposition.

Surely it can be no coincidence that the decade of the sixties also saw the burgeoning of television tournament athletics, primarily professional and college football, that strange marriage of the twentieth century to the Middle Ages where the heraldic animal team mascots are a direct transference from medieval coats of arms. Football, along with the news, shared the virtue of being "live," and it also boasted that further amplification of reality: instant replay.

Certainly no other form of imagination mechanism has yet been found to equal the power of televised football for the American male. Heretofore seemingly backward in spiritual matters, he has finally had his potential for ecstasy and commitment unlocked by the Super Bowl. Unmoved by magazine photographs of malnourished children in South America, increasingly calloused to printed pricks to his political conscience, he has been moved to tears and prayer by the sight of an intercepted twenty-yard pass on television.

Observe that it is not just football that did the trick, but televised football. Most fans will tell you they prefer to watch a game on television rather than attend the actual event. The usual reason given is that they can see better. Quite true. The average camera work on a professional football game is astounding in its virtuosity. In the stands, even on the fifty-yard line, one is limited by actual distance, the surrounding crowds, the lack of a running commentary. Even the instant replay now projected on giant screens in the stadium does not satisfy. The scale is all wrong.

The players themselves never see the game as well as the TV-viewer. In fact, at least one college player who was a first round draft choice this year admits to never having seen a live professional game at all. What is provided the homebound fan is a god's-eye view of the game. Close-ups of the tension in the coach's face, distance shots of the ball hurtling through space, replays from various angles of the runback. By such divine privilege is the passion of the soul unlocked.

It was then through a series of "historical events," chiefly the assassinations of the sixties, the attempted assassinations of the seventies, the riots, the war, and finally the gargantuan, slow motion disaster of Watergate, coupled with the ahistorical event of football, that real life (otherwise known as "live action") was wedded to movie-life with undreamed of repercussions in the American consciousness. With a subtle ontological reversal, what was real became what was televisable.

There is a certain democratizing in this process. Not only are presidents and Senate subcommittees real, but so is the wife slain by her jealous husband. And strikes. And muscular dystrophy. And talk show guests. Even diapers and garbage. The success of soap operas is simple. They have elevated the life of the housewife to the realm of reality by televising interiors. Practically all daytime television takes place inside a building, whereas a good portion of evening entertainment is filmed outside. With the important exception of situation comedy. It is instructive that all commercials about diapers or garbage bags are either miniature soap operas or short comic skits. Thus all of life, even toothbrushing, has finally been sanctified through incarnation on television.

But Sontag's dictum that every era must reinvent its own spirituality is catching up with television. What was to have been the first full-fledged television generation has predictably apostatized. What has power over the fathers' imaginations draws a blank with the children. They couldn't tell a Senate subcommittee from the starting lineup of the Detroit Lions and wouldn't see the point in trying.

There is currently a lot of handwringing over resurgent student apathy because young people no longer do all those deplorable but televisable things they did in the sixties. They watch neither the six o'clock news nor Monday night football. They are thereby denying the significant reality, the spirituality of their parents.

They are instead ensconced in their private citadels of sound, either hooked up to headphones in their bedrooms or cruising in an automobile equipped with a tape deck and stereophonic speakers. But this accounts for only their private devotional time. Corporate spirituality is accomplished through "live" concerts where the musicians are actually in the same geographical area as the audience, although only through electronics are they audibly accessible.

The children will go to a great deal more trouble to attend a live concert than their fathers will to attend a live football game. Dad somehow senses his soul mates, an invisible cloud of witnesses, gathered around the tube on Monday night to share his passion. Yet his children feel the need for physical solidarity, to actually see and touch the host encamped around the priests and priestesses who mediate their shared spirituality. Just as the point of attending a "real" football game is lost on dad, so his suggestion to his children that they spend their money on a record album instead of a ticket puzzles them.

There is no denying the fact that these public, often outdoor, concerts are the highlight of the devotees' experience. This is partly owing to the nature of music itself; "live" music has always been preferred, even by fans of Lawrence Welk. However, the electronics necessary to an open air concert considerably alters the quality of what used to be called "live" music. The performer holds the microphone like a metallic ice cream cone. An instrumentalist fiddles knowingly with the knobs on his amplifier. Yet part of the total experience of the performance consists precisely in how the microphone is held and the amplifier controlled. In other words, the musician's interaction with the electronics. Perhaps one has to see this part of the performance in order to reproduce it in the mind's eye when a recording of the concert's music is played in privacy at home.

Here it would seem we had completed the cycle and were back to the same point of the darkened movie theatre where one is impregnated with images that are then carried home and worked into an interior theatre of the mind. In many ways this is true. The musicians wear costumes much more elaborate and flashy than Ann Blyth ever dreamed of. The audience projects itself onto the stage, yearns to become a part of that action, sometimes orgiastic, sometimes romantic. But the music, once no more than a background component of the movies, has now become the central focus. The performers are characters. They are not simply anon-

ymous figures like the players in a symphony orchestra, all
indistinguishable in their frumpy dark suits and dresses.
The clothes, the hairdos, the motions are all meant to con-
vey a particular character to the audience.

But a character in what? This is where the similarity
between movies and music ends. The performers are characters in their own music, not in any plotted story. Alice
Cooper is the Surrealistic Madman. John Denver is the
Ecology Kid. What they live is not story but something
called life-style.

The point is obvious: music is abstract, amorphous long-
ing while movies are sharp-edged, concrete, and therefore
limited by definition. True, media music almost always has
words and the words are important. But they do not make
up a story, a ballad. Rather, they are poetry, occasionally
of a high order, but fragmentary and lyrical. Coherence and
continuity is of negative value; mood and mystification is
the creative intent.

So, after the concert, the devotee descends from his ecstasy, buys the group's current album, goes home and plays
it until he has it memorized. Not just the words, although
that sometimes takes some doing, but every musical coun-
terpoint, every intonation and eccentric pronunciation of
the singer.

Marshall McLuhan has called the technology of the
phonograph a "music hall without walls." Is this why, despite the severe acoustical problems, the "live" concerts are
preferably held out of doors, in parks, football stadiums,
even pastures? Why is it that these sorts of concerts have
not translated well to television? The TV musical comedy
acts of such performers as Donny and Marie Osmond never
call forth the same sort of spiritual participation that the
concerts or records do.

In a recent television special, "The Making of Star Wars,"
we were told that a sign of that film's great success and
impact on our culture was the way it spilled over into other
media. Star Wars T-shirts, posters, toys, records, Halloween
costumes, Christmas gifts, and bumper stickers prolifer-
ated. Any highly successful media production now seems to

radiate outward, supplying energy for other modes of expression. The television production *about* a movie production is the newest discovery of how to feed one medium with another.

For it is a very important point that within American culture, contrary to the inferences originally drawn from McLuhan's work on media, no mode of communication seems to drop into obsolescence. People are not reading fewer books because of television. Nor has it killed the movie industry, although it precipitated considerable revamping of its techniques. Radio is still ubiquitous. Newspapers and magazines, despite their struggle with postal rates and paper prices, survive. Posters, drawing on the content of books, records, television, and movies, and taking the form of miniature billboards, have given us our dominant graphic style. Instead of rivalry between various forms of media, we have an unprecedented interplay between them. They bolster and protect one another.

Thus the tentacles of popular culture reach out to us all in an inescapable embrace, defining not simply our shared values but something that is prior to values, our shared way of perceiving the world. Real life exists in the shared technological sensory extensions of ourselves. Human activity is real for us only insofar as it participates in those shared sensations. To open a nationally advertised brand of soup is to share a communion deeply satisfying to our psyches. We are suddenly confident; we are nationally affirmed by everyone from the Campbell Soup Kids fo Andy Warhol.

Nevertheless, so unaware are we of the way our culture shapes us that Christians assume it is only with well-labelled vices and virtues that we must contend. Adultery versus chastity. Homosexuality versus heterosexuality. Embezzling versus honesty. "Bad" language versus "good." But what, electronically speaking, is bad or good communication? Is it all neutral? Does God inexplicably prefer aborigines, innocent of technological media, to the neurologically extended Westerner as he had that puzzling predilection for Abel over Cain?

Our problem with culture is a frighteningly new one. Despite our genuine nostalgia for being fed to the lions or burned at the stake, those are, unfortunately, no longer our options. Even the Buddhist monks of the sixties who resorted to burning themselves alive failed to fire our imaginations. Our culture has become cautious of making martyrs of its enemies. Our struggle with our society is this: how to escape being sucked into the media vortex the way particles of light are drawn irresistibly into the magnetic force field of a black hole.

It is not enough merely to be aware of the problem—a weak solution McLuhan proposed in his first book, *The Mechnical Bride*. With awareness comes a critical attitude towards one's culture, McLuhan said. And with criticism the capacity to accept or reject. Whether McLuhan himself any longer thought that solution tenable by the time he wrote *Understanding Media* is uncertain. But as he deftly pointed out in the beginning of that book, "it is no time to suggest strategies when the threat has not even been acknowledged to exist."

He, of course, defined the threat as an assault on rational man's freedom from manipulation by the media, the control of which is bought and sold as lucrative commodities in technological markets. However, our concern is somewhat different here. Certainly individuals and families must wrestle with the effects of media upon themselves. But the temptation for the corporate Christian establishment, whether ecclesiastical or otherwise, has been even more insidious. It has been overjoyed at and entirely uncritical of its novel opportunities to become media manipulator itself, a bidder in the competition to control these commodities.

It is as though we had been told we could make a bundle for the Kingdom by smuggling cocaine or transporting slaves and had eagerly cornered the market without considering the relative righteousness of such means. Certain that the content of our message was irreproachable, we have given no thought to the form it took, other than to check its effectiveness with marketing analysts. While we have been morally incensed at the contemporary slogan "If it feels good, do it," we have unconsciously adopted the equally reprehensible "If it works, do it."

All kinds of questionable methods work: coercion, torture, extortion, brainwashing. Unfortunately, almost all of them have been used at one time or another by some religious body. Also fortunately, or rather graciously, most of them have eventually been revealed as unworthy servants. We now look back with mingled horror and regret at the Constantinian alliance of the church and state, at the Spanish Inquisition, at the wars of religion that scarred the Reformation. How will history view our own accommodation to culture? Have we in this era left the reinvention of spirituality to Simon the magician who would buy and sell the power of the Holy Spirit? Have we given over the creating of plans "aimed at resolving the painful structural contradictions inherent in the human situation, at the completion of human consciousness, at transcendence" to Walt Disney and ITT? Is the imagination and genius of the Christian church so depleted that it can only copy the metaphysical models offered by the movies?

It is time we, quite literally, got hold of ourselves, like the adolescent stumbling back into the light of day from the dark theater who must begin again to grapple with the reality he would gladly trade for an illusion. And to begin with the first step McLuhan advocates, that is, simple awareness, let us look at several instances of uncritical if effective media manipulation with evangelistic intentions, remembering with what innocent-appearing bricks the road to perdition is paved.

Chapter III:

THE TOTAL IMAGE

"You are really important to me. Therefore, I have compiled the enclosed material especially for you."—Billy Zeoli in an advertising brochure from Gospel Films

ERNEST DICHTER, GENERALLY ACKNOWLEDGED as the inventor of image advertising, advised one of his associates that the "best technique for selling is to paint for the customer a total picture of the kind of person he would like to be, and then make him believe your product is a necessary part of that picture" (Sally Helgesen, "Virtue Rewarded," *Harper's*, May, 1978, p. 23). For this reason automobile ads display their product in the most unlikely places—on glistening beaches or in verdant meadows, all traces of tire tracks erased. The youthful Scotch drinker profiled in the latest glossy magazine is pictured in his study surrounded by hardback books, the shadowy interior revealing glimpses of Persian carpet, leather upholstery, healthy pot plants, chrome track lighting, an Aran Isle sweater, and a registered retriever.

My teetotalling parents often pointed out to me in my youth the insidiousness of such advertising. It was the favorite topic of my logic professor in college. I harangued my own students about its perils to clear, objective thinking. But the beauty part of image advertising is that the audience can be aware of the ruse yet still affected by it. Catching on to the gimmick does not make us immune to the infection. Despite our most rationally disapproving selves, we still lust after the image in the picture.

The damage does not stop there, however. So potent is the underlying concept of image advertising that the very people who decry its use in the marketplace of consumer goods unquestioningly make use of it to sell their own ideologies and causes. Certain feminists, for example, have found the most convincing way of converting women to their cause is through image advertising. They seek to replace the picture of the frumpy old maid who lives down the street and digs dandelions out of the lawn in rubber galoshes and her housecoat with the snappy image of a career woman, dressed to the teeth, carrying a designer briefcase stuffed with airline tickets to Acapulco and birth control pills. The fact that the old maid may indeed be the more independent of the two is irrelevant, just as it is unimportant that a high percentage of Scotch drinkers may be middle-aged, slovenly failures.

Psychologists and education theorists tell us we must have a good "self-image" in order to function properly. With that as our behavioral basis, we ourselves become a consumer product, a component in the ad space. We do not need to be good in fact and substance, only in image. In this way we are able to sell ourselves to others—employers, spouses, friends—and even ultimately to ourselves.

The Christian media have, like the rest of the culture, inadvertently taken up the same techniques. Driven by a laudable response to the call of the Great Commission, they have used the most effective model for communication they know—image advertising. Its success makes old-fashioned apologetics look like an archaeological oddity. Catechisms are replaced by conferences on life-style.

Culture is not a planned process. It evolves, like a river finding its course, from the common understandings, resources, and desires of a people. No one foresaw our susceptibility to image advertising. The ad men themselves only picked up on the unprecedented proliferation of communications media and stumbled into success. No one planned that Christianity could be sold like any other consumer product. Our minds were simply predisposed that way by our culture. And since we find ourselves wandering here in the midst of this fairyland of technology, why not take advantage of it? Or as Bruce Cook, the former advertising agent for Coca-Cola who engineered the "I found it" campaign, put it, "Back in Jerusalem when the church started,

God performed a miracle there on the Day of Pentecost. They didn't have the benefit of buttons and media, so God had to do a little supernatural work there. But today, with our technology, we have available to us the opportunity to create the same kind of interest in a secular society" (Arthur Unger, " 'Born Again' Phenomenon," *Christian Science Monitor*, July 13, 1977).

"The same kind of interest"? I don't think so. The account in Acts describes the spectators at Pentecost as first "amazed" and "in doubt," then "mocking." Following Peter's sermon they were "pricked in the heart" and "fear came upon every soul." Admittedly, I have heard some people mock the "I found it" bumper stickers, going so far as to plaster their own bumpers with retaliatory stickers bearing the message "I lost it." Many others simply expressed doubt of either the sincerity or the sanctity of the self-proclaimed finders. But amazed, pricked, or fearful I have not observed. Instead of the interest being parallel to that at Pentecost, it more nearly approximates the interest shown in a visiting football team.

That particular media blitz, indeed practically every attempt by Christians to "create interest," which is after all only a euphemism for advertising, has been based on the appeal of image advertising. We have learned not to spell out "Jesus Saves" with whitewashed rocks on the side of the road. That approach is not only embarrassingly backward but ineffective. Instead, bit by bit, object by object, the picture of Christian, no longer with Bunyan's backpack and staff, but in a basketball uniform or a three-piece executive suit, is put before us. The point is to make the picture so appealing that the customer wants to see himself within the frame. Health, wealth, youth (or at least youthful age), sharp clothes, exuberant optimism. Is the product Coca-Cola or Christ? It's hard to tell.

Actually, the product is life-style, that loathsome word that has succeeded in trivializing our existence for us. It is a necessary component in the wardrobe of someone with a good self-image. One opens the closet, puts on his life-style, looks in the mirror, and there's his self-image smiling at him.

Why does every Christian self-help book have a photograph of the happy couple that spawned it on the jacket, grinning cozily from their suburban lawn? Why does every inspirational book have daisies draped beside a cup of coffee? Why does Cliff Barrows intone the final benediction to Johnny Cash's Easter Special filmed in Israel from a book-lined study with a massive mahogany desk and a crackling fire? Let us be honest. For the same reason that Dewar's Scotch pays young professionals to pose in casually elegant surroundings.

The product that Mr. Cook and other Christian advertisers are supposedly selling is Christ. Yet Christ is nowhere to be found in the picture. If he were, it would severely limit the marketing potential of the picture. Christ is motivationally equivalent to, say, Geritol. Any ad man knows there is no point in putting out a picture of a bottle of Geritol. Instead, he shows a picture of a youthful, happily married couple who attribute their health and success to Geritol. The same with Jesus. He himself doesn't sell well, any more than a bottle of tonic. So the ad shows pictures of people who can testify to the therapeutic results in their lives. The appeal is the same as in any image advertisement: put yourself in this picture.

Let us look in more detail now at some of the experimental attempts to sell Christ to our culture, whether this is called evangelism or making the gospel relevant to our world. In either case the underlying premise is Bruce Cook's—we must "create interest."

The PTL Club comes on at 5:30 in the morning. Several people in my community watch it regularly. Most of them are elderly widows who rise early from habit and no longer have anyone to keep them company at that hour of the day. But there are also a couple of families who make it part of their morning routine. They find it entertaining in much the same way other early risers enjoy "Good Morning America." The PTL Club, however, speaks their language whereas the secular morning talk shows make them uneasy.

The format of the PTL Club, though, leans more heavily on Johnny Carson's Tonight Show than the morning man-woman team shows. The entrance of the host, in fact, with the fanfare and the initial monologue, is lifted almost wholly from Johnny Carson. There is even a chubby, laughing corresponding number who plays Ed McMahon, the foil for the host. The host himself is nattily dressed and has blow-dried hair. He has replaced Carson's air of world-weariness with an ambience that wanders between intense jollity and repressed seriousness. One could never reproach this Christian with being long-faced.

As on most host-talk shows, the content consists primarily of what is in the trade called "promo." All the people who gradually fill up the line of seats next to the host have something—a book, a record, a film, a concert—to promote. The host helps them do this. He displays copies of the book, lends them his studio orchestra to accompany them in a sample song, visits via videotape the set being built for another new Christian television program.

Then the host has something to promote himself. It is a new subsidiary venture of the PTL Club, a Christian camp and retreat center near Ft. Heritage, North Carolina, called the Total Image Center. We see taped highlights of the land being cleared and "chalets" going up. There are, the host informs us, half a million dollars' worth of bulldozers currently working it over. Attached to the Total Image Center is a School of Evangelism where lay people will be taught how to effectively spread the Gospel. The Total Image Center will cost, the host estimates, $100 million.

We switch back to the studio where the host shows us a five-volume set of home Bible studies, developed by the curriculum coordinator for Oral Roberts University. They are a gift to anyone who calls the toll-free number during the show and pledges $100 to the completion of the Total Image Center.

Since this show, unlike Carson's, is for family consumption, there is something for the kiddies too, a hand-puppet skit. The characters are a little girl and her dog, both irrepressibly obstreperous. In fact, a little more obstreperous than the host seems comfortable with. They too, it appears, are soon to have their own show. One gets the impression that the host will not be sorry to see them go, although the live audience has found them amusing. At length the host is able to insert his daily children's sermon into the antics of the puppets. The question is, he says, what does being spiritual mean? After some good-natured banter, the three agree that being spiritual is *not* going to church and putting in your offering. Rather it is, in the precise words of the host, "being nice." At that he moves on quickly to the next guest before the puppets have a chance to grow unruly again.

The next guest is a well-known Christian songwriter. He does not sing although he does display one of his new hymnals which incorporates sacred songs from every currently popular genre. He and the host discuss the lingering prejudices of some Christians toward the adoption of secular musical styles into a church setting. They agree that the church, by and large, has become stodgy and ineffectual. What is needed is more contemporary music to attract the ungodly. "If it works, let's do it," the composer proposes. The host concurs. They also agree that if the church had been doing its job well in the past, they—the songwriter and the host—would not have to be on nationwide television at this moment, doing its job for it. However, the church has failed, or at any rate faltered, in its mission, and they have picked up the ball.

Following this exchange of ideas there is a musical number, one of the guest's composing, by the regular PTL Singers, who are young and brisk. They are artfully arranged, some sitting on steps, some standing in clusters. They wear long dresses and tuxedos. If they lack that certain *élan* that makes Donny and Marie so appealing to the preteen set, they nevertheless appear overwhelmingly happy and in good health, the sort of kids Christian parents pray for.

As the show draws to a close, the host gives us a brief pep talk about the expanding resources of the PTL Club. There will shortly be a PTL satellite which will make it possible to export the program to every continent and to import on-the-spot interviews with PTL-approved missionaries around the globe. The audience applauds. The camera scans the faces. They look to be for the most part good, kind, happy faces. They are applauding, the host is grinning goodbye, the band is playing. There is a commercial for Century 21 Real Estate agencies. With a start one realizes the show is over.

The PTL Club has a lot in common with the Oral Roberts Specials which occur at least twice every year, at Christmas and Easter. The production is consequently a little slicker. It comes closer to approximating The Donny and Marie Show than Johnny Carson or Howdy Doody. The singers are racially balanced, the sets more sophisticated in the Peter Max poster style. The guest star is from the secular world, always a featured coup in these enterprises.

The guest star for Easter 1978 is Vikki Carr. The master of ceremonies is Oral's son, Richard. He is handsome in a baby-faced way with a streak of grey down his pompadour that one cannot resist speculating about. (Hair seems almost symbolic in all these productions. The silver sculpture-cut of the host of the West Coast celebrity interview show "High Adventure" inspires genuine awe.) Richard seems guileless and winning as he sings, introduces, and "chats" with the guest star on Perry Como stools.

Like the PTL Club, the Oral Roberts Specials have a live audience, frequently scanned by the camera. The softcore gospel songs are skillfully arranged. The singers are good, good enough for secular television, one cannot help observing with relief. For this is prime time, not 5:30 in the morning when only devotees will be watching.

Vikki Carr sings too. She certainly has no problem with *élan*. With the sound off or the words blurred, one could tell no difference between her delivery here or on any secular variety show. There is the same pantomime of passion, the identical intense body language. The *tête-à-tête* with Richard that follows, in case anyone has gotten the wrong idea, is about the "charity work" she does, promoting scholarships for disadvantaged Hispanic students. In her own way, Vikki is every bit as winning as Richard. What she does, she does well and without any of the overweening ego that is visible in many guest stars.

But now the entertainment part of the show is over. Even Vikki takes her place in the pew alongside Oral's Evelyn. Richard and singers disappear from the set. Everyone settles down for the *pièce de resistance*.

Oral Roberts' style is now avuncular. Maybe that goes with being a Methodist. Gone are the blood, sweat, and tears of his days as the faith healer on Sunday morning television. He is dressed not as a dandy but as a dapper uncle should be, which means pinstripes instead of his son's ascot. The fire, the drama, the passion of the old days have all been toned down. Still, he stands behind one of the stools left on stage from the chat set, gripping its sides like a pulpit.

From time to time he has trouble with the cameras. He slips into preaching to the audience and forgets his camera full-face. An unseen stagehand cues him and he once again focuses forward, startled and momentarily disconcerted. One wonders why, having been on television almost as long as Ed Sullivan, he still seems a novice with the medium. Interwoven in his sermons are stories that have only the most tenuous ties to his theme. One is about a pony and one is a fish story of the old school. He tells them with so much animation that the cameraman is hard pressed to keep up with him. The old rascal has managed to sanctify his Oklahoma heritage of storytelling by slipping them into a sermon.

Afterwards there is a filmed appeal for his new Tulsa hospital project. Then a final number, following the traditional worship pattern if not the style, by the singers, Richard, and Vikki. Last of all, the Oral Roberts signature, the quickening proclamation of I John 4:4: "Greater is he that is in you than he that is in the world." This one sentence has a peculiar electrifying effect, no matter how one feels about all that has gone before.

There is an important difference between these specials and the televised "crusades" of Billy Graham. First of all, there is more blatant entertainment value in the specials, a fact indicated by their very name. The crusades are not

put together to be entertaining even though they too utilize
the guest star technique. Celebrities from the secular world
are again a prize plum to be displayed for the encouragement of the faithful and the abashment of the infidels. B. J.
Thomas endorses Jesus as Bruce Jenner endorses cereal.
The logical non sequitur affronts the viewer in both cases.
Why should one consume either Jesus or Wheaties just because a celebrity does? In order to magically participate in
their prowess and fame? Actually Bruce Jenner has the better case. The inference is that eating Wheaties will contribute to one's being a champion like Jenner. But what is the
covert claim of Christian celebrities? Why wouldn't the testimony of some nameless drug-addict have the same effect?
Do Christian media events rely so heavily on famous con-
verts because their experience is more authentic than that
of the anonymous believer? Or is it, again, just a gimmick
to "create interest"?

At any rate, the stars appear at the crusades primarily
for their endorsement rather than their entertainment value.
Billy Graham has his own troupe of professional musicians
trained in the old school of stand-up-and-sing-straight. There
is no hint of soft-shoe, no monkeying around with the hand-
held mike. There is even "congregational singing," although
this has diminished during the past few years. One verse of
one hymn is usually all the audience is allowed. Representa-
tive local church choirs, however, provide the background
music for the invitation. And when Billy preaches, it is behind an identifiable pulpit with a slack-bound Bible in hand
and *to* the audience. There are few concessions to the camera, which maintains a respectful attitude of simply cap-
turing the action instead of creating it.

While Oral Roberts has acceded to the format of entertainment, Billy Graham has by and large kept the format
of a church service, although admittedly it is stretched to
the breaking point by the size of the auditorium or stadium,
the number of people involved, and the electronic hazards
of lights, cables, and sound systems. Interestingly enough,
though, the camera now cuts out during the first verse of
the invitation hymn. The action is over.

Still, one can see just how far we have moved in pack-
aging the product, even though the content ostensibly remains the same, from the PTL Club to the Billy Graham
Evangelistic Crusades. Shows such as the PTL Club, High
Adventure, the Oral Roberts or Johnny Cash or Pat Boone
Specials, are put together with the express intention of com-
peting for the nation's leisure time. Billy Graham's Crusades, relying on their substantial heritage and the drawing
power of the preacher's reputation, are bald revival meetings, with no attempt to disguise the fact.

Such a shift in format has resulted in the fecundity of
a whole new enterprise in Christendom—the Christian entertainment industry. Bible bookstores are now papered with
announcements of Christian concerts instead of revival
meetings. The supposition is that the gospel will be more
palatable if it is placed in the secularly appealing setting of
staged entertainment. Rather than amateur hymn-singing
and a sermon which bores believers and unbelievers alike,
the production is musical from one end to the other, with a
certain amount of personal testimony interspersed between
numbers. Sometimes there is a single performer, sometimes
a group and a band. The more famous the main attraction,
the nearer to emulating a secular concert the production
gets, going so far as to have a warm-up group, followed later
in the evening by the drawing card. The lighting, the sets,
the sound system must all be professionally managed. Ad-
mission is charged, although for lesser known performers it
is often called a donation. After the concert there are sometimes records on sale in the lobby.

Christian record companies are perhaps the fastest pro-
liferating segment of the Christian entertainment industry.
Tapes and records take up a growing area of the average
Christian bookstore. For the musician enjoying even a mod-
icum of success on the Christian circuit, this soon means an
agent to handle all his bookings and promote him with the
record companies. The top agencies wield a great deal of
power in the business. Not only do they decide the sort of
music that will be contracted, but they also act as spiritual
arbiter to their clients, often shaping their theology as well

as their careers. And the musicians are under considerable pressure to accept the agent's decrees. After all, he is the one with his knowledgable finger on the pulse of his public. He knows whether hallelujahs and praise-the-lords are still in or not.

And that public, whether they are most turned on by *Godspell* or the Gaithers, are ever more willing to see these productions as entertainment rather than evangelism. Christian concerts are their special preserve, their counter to the secular culture's unacceptable acts. The latest outgrowth of the Christian entertainment industry, then, is Christian nightclubs. Since the economic undergirding for nightclubs has always been overpriced alcohol, these Christian clubs have found themselves forced to charge outrageous sums for soft drinks, but their clientele seems willing to pay as long as the total experience adequately duplicates that of its secular counterpart.

To an outsider it must often seem that what commercial Christianity is promoting is a certain certified life-style, one that has little to do with dusty feet or lilies of the field. In some circles the proper insignia are white buck shoes and friendly football players. In other circles it's liberation and lettuce boycotts. In either case, what are selected from the really rather meager offering of "life-styles" in the shop windows of our world are only copies of designer originals. One shops around for a few years in the ready-to-wear department, supposedly searching for the life-style that fits him best. He may find his choice a little tight and restricted through the shoulders, but since any individual is ultimately more pliable than a cultural norm, he will eventually shrink to fit it. Fewer and fewer homemade lives appear in public and Christians have to be particularly careful to avoid deviations from cultural fashions. The last thing in the world we want is to appear tacky.

Life-style workshops are the means by which we learn how to make the necessary alterations and adjustments. Whatever style one opts for in one's life, there is a semiar somewhere that will show you how to fit it. You can learn how to be a Total Woman or an OK guy. There is prosperity training for the Christian businessman and assertiveness training for the Christian feminist. Cooking for Christians and dieting for Christians. Salvation through solar energy and effective parenthood.

All of these demand a certain prearranged stance towards life. The life-style shopper "buys into" the chosen fashion in much the same way and for the same reason that he opts for polyester double knit or prewashed denim. And the lines of demarcation between the styles, even though both consider themselves Christian, are not friendly frontiers. A certified feminist in her peasant blouse and jeans does not fit among the Total Woman in peignoirs. An OK guy cannot function as a Bill Gothard father. However, all of these can blend inconspicuously into the surroundings of their secular counterparts. Any Total Woman can easily be Miss—or Mrs.—America. In fact, she probably aspires to that distinction. And any OK guy will be everybody's favorite buddy at the Racquet Club.

An unbeliever, supplied with only the picture of the product that these life-style workshops present, would not have an inkling that the original pattern these people profess to imitate was a vagrant celibate whose own seminar on happiness elevated the mourning meek rather than the smiling success. Yet whether it is a seminary jockeying for a spot at the Aspen Institute for Humanistic Studies or an Athletes in Action training camp, the image of impeccable cultural accommodation is the goal.

One wonders how the wife of an alcoholic whose family is falling apart around her feels when she sees the Celebrity Christmas Special with its apotheosis of the happy Christian family. How does the migrant worker, hundreds of miles from home, feel when he looks out the school bus window at the sprightly smile of the fellow on the billboard who's found it? How does an old maid nearing senility respond to the good news that she's okay? Life-style for them is not a matter of shopping around. Life is what they live. They take whatever is thrust at them day by day.

According to some accounts, advertising has been the largest component of the social revolution in this country.

Poor people saw and lusted after what they supposed to be the common lot of all average Americans. The sexually repressed and timid were bombarded with ideals of beautiful, accessible bodies. People everywhere began to expect and demand what they presumed everyone else had.

The same dynamic seems to be operating among Christians. They are universally pictured as successful, svelte, and integrated. Our current notions of both evangelism and edification are borrowed from image advertising. The meek, the misfit, the poor in spirit, the suffering servant are not allowed inside the picture.

Chapter IV:

THE GROTESQUE GOSPEL

*"In fact we should never ask of anything 'Is it real?',
for everything is real. The proper question is 'A real
what?'"* —C. S. Lewis

THE PURPOSE OF EVERY media presentation, whether
television program, newspaper story, training film,
or billboard, is to persuade us to accept as real the
world we see focused through its lens. While actually
in the business of begetting and nursing fantasies about
ourselves, the intent of a soap opera or a political slogan is
to have its product embraced as what matters in the world.
The purpose of the proclamation of the Gospel, on the other
hand, is to draw attention to the rift between conventionally
accepted reality and the reality of Christ. Through the technological mesh of shared sensation we are asked to affirm
the overriding significance of a coal strike, lemon-scented
detergent, the migration of caribou, the neutron bomb, rev-
olutionary sex, and dubbed music. Whether one approves of
any or all of these products is irrelevant. The point is not
approval or disapproval, but only our acceptance of them as
what makes up real life. One can be for the development of
the neutron bomb and use a different brand of detergent.
Still one accepts this media package as what is important
about life. The issues—life's issues—are culturally agreed
upon by their presentation to our extended technological
awareness, whether those issues are presented discursively
through "the news" and magazines or narratively through
Charlie's Angels and the latest hit record.

The coal miners in Appalachia go on strike. Reporters
and technicians arrive to record the event. In the life of the
small town, the presence of the media personnel suddenly
becomes more absorbing than the strike itself. The men

hang around the grocery store and the service station, shy but eager to be interviewed by the man with the microphone. One of them, who up to now has been most concerned with how he's going to make his mortgage payment and buy groceries, is asked for his opinion about the negotiation deadline. Now he feels that if the interview makes it to the national network, the entire strike will have been worth it. Immortality will be his. His life will be real, normative, validated human existence.

The reporters and cameramen are extremely adept at their job. They maneuver to get the off-guard expression that will reveal the essence of Striking Minerhood. Sometimes this must be contrived, but that is only natural since the miners find it difficult to "be themselves" with the camera rolling. Suddenly they can only be people pretending to be miners. The selves they try to be have inexplicably evaporated. Where has the reality gone? Why has the whole town become something it's not? The cameraman is familiar with the phenomenon. He has seen it happen, not just with the miners, but with politicians, guerillas, African tribal chiefs, and migrant workers. He has spent years trying to create a truly candid camera. Yet reality always recedes just over the horizon when he appears. "Act natural," he continually tells his subjects, and it seems that he is the only one who recognizes the contradictory command as a joke.

The experiment with televising the Loud family a few years ago in its natural habitat ended with the evaporation of everybody. Where once there had been a family, however ramshackle, only a haunted house was left.

The camera cannot catch reality any more than (and perhaps less than) the painter. Indeed, it was this very dilemma that enthralled the cubist painters of the early twentieth century. What they wanted, they announced to the world, was to paint not what they could see, but what they knew was there, lurking beneath the deceptive membrane of visibility.

It is with what the camera cannot hope to catch, with what it in fact drives away, that the gospel is concerned. Therein lies our trial. As creatures of our culture, we will accept as real only what can be shared through the electronic extension of our senses. Any data that are not considered significant enough to be fed into that network or that, by their very nature, are incapable of being transmitted through the network, become for us, *ipso facto*, unreal. Anything requiring directly apprehended, unmediated experience cannot be successfully fed into that network. It remains in the pile of rejected possibilities that the cameraman leaves behind when he packs up his gear and leaves town.

Malcolm Muggeridge says that the danger of the video medium is that by its very nature it presents a narrow, manipulated excerpt of film as reality. "It's very nearly impossible to tell the truth in television. . . . Putting it in simplest terms, if I write a novel, signed by my name, I am saying these are my thoughts, these are my views, these are my impressions, and the response of the reader is according. If you set up a camera and take a film, that is not considered to be anybody's views: that is reality" (*Christ and the Media*, Eerdmans, p. 106).

We take it as reality for the simple but understandable reason that these are not mental pictures formed by our own imagination as they are when we read a book or even listen to the radio, but are pictures of actual human bodies, walking and talking. The electronically transmitted images are somehow more real, even if only black and white, than our own internally generated mental images. Is it because they are being simultaneously shared with millions of other viewers while the pictures of our own mind's eye can be validated by no one else? If each of us had a secret TV set that broadcast programs exclusively to us, programs no one else could see, would we bother to watch or would we be so overwhelmed with the anguish of its incommunicability that the secret set would become only an irritant, a constant reminder of our special isolation? Remember: no one else could see what we were seeing, be moved as we were by our visions. If we tried to tell someone else, to describe our solitary experiences, we would be under a great, almost insupportable burden of language.

For all but the most desperately tenacious, the impulse would be to ignore more and more the private TV set, to turn it to the wall if one could not succeed in unplugging it altogether, and in its place to pay more and more attention to the shared sensations that hook up millions of viewers to New York and to one another. So little explanation is needed there. Only a few code words and the meaning is passed. "Did you watch Johnny Carson last night?" Instantly the file is flipped, the shared memory retrieved. Or "What do you think about the coal strike?" Again, a data bank of mutually received bits of information distributed nationally is drawn upon for the response.

Each of us, of course, has the secret camera. From time to time we give it our attention, are caught by a particularly engrossing scene that flashes across the screen. But unfortunately, there are no reruns on that channel. The sun will never set in quite that way again. "Look now. See it!" we may insist to the person who is with us. But what is one person, or four? The whole experience is negligible when compared to the photographed sensation shared by four million. It is those four million who validate our experience as genuine. We *know* it happened. Four million people can't be wrong.

The private experience is illusory. It slips away, not into an imperishable film cannister, but into our own quite perishable memories. For ages the race has had to rely on the primitive mechanism of the collective unconscious. Now we have detailed documentation of our shared sensations. Who will have the effrontery to suggest that reality resides in private, isolated screenings rather than the mutually validated sensory network?

Walker Percy, in his book *The Message in the Bottle*, reminds us of an unsettling aspect of our reliance on mediated experience:

> García López de Cárdenas discovered the Grand Canyon and was amazed at the sight. It can be imagined: One crosses miles of desert, breaks through the mesquite, and there it is at one's feet. Later the government set the place aside as a

national park, hoping to pass along to millions the experience of Cárdenas. . . .

The assumption is that the Grand Canyon is a remarkably interesting and beautiful place and that if it had a certain value P for Cárdenas, the same value P may be transmitted to any number of sightseers. . . . A counterinfluence is at work, however, and it would be nearer the truth to say that if the place is seen by a million sightseers, a single sightseer does not receive value P but a millionth part of value P. . . .

Why is it almost impossible to gaze directly at the Grand Canyon under these circumstances and see it for what it is— as one picks up a strange object from one's back yard and gazes directly at it? (pp. 46-47)

His answer is that the experience of the Grand Canyon has been appropriated by the very mechanism meant to mediate the experience to millions. All the geography books, the postcards, the travel brochures, the television documentaries, have been heaped up to form an impenetrable barrier between us and the Grand Canyon. We cannot possibly see the Grand Canyon in the same way that Cárdenas did. The Grand Canyon has been "preformulated" for us in a way that precludes our actual confrontation with it. All that can happen now, short of a catastrophe which would rip away the wrapping, is a matching of our perceptions with the media-package labelled "Grand Canyon." If our perceptions coincide, we feel relieved and satisfied, the contemporary form of catharsis. The canyon has lived up to its press, our preformulated expectations. If something untoward intervenes, if the day is overcast and the colors do not glow as we have been led to expect, we are uneasy and feel cheated of the promised experience.

It is impossible to overstate, yet necessary for us to understand and to feel fully, just how much our experience of life today is determined and modified by the media. Imagine taking a vacation—like Marco Polo—to some place you had never seen photographs of. It is unthinkable. Who would want to? What would be the point? Our experience *must* be mediated, preformulated for us, or else we feel totally disoriented. Remove the media context from our lives and we would become monsters. We would confront the world directly and would have no idea what to do with it. It would terrorize rather than delight us.

Yet it is with that reality that flees from the camera and with that secret television screen that the Gospel is concerned. And it is precisely the unphotographable fugitive fact and the isolated set that constitutes the grotesque in our time. Although grotesque has grown connotations of repulsive or ugly, it has also historically meant "fantastically extravagant" or "ludicrously incongruous." God becoming man, for example. The glory of the cross. The resurrection of the body. All are paradoxes, and the nature of paradox is the grotesque.

We need not think that the central paradox of our own predicament is peculiar to contemporary culture. The elusive, and therefore rejected, reality becoming the truly significant was put into architectural terms by Jesus: "the stone which the builders rejected, the same is become the head of the corner." We have simply switched the manner and metaphor of rejection.

The Gospel is grotesque. We have got to give in to that idea, no matter how repulsive, no matter how—and especially because—it goes against every culturally conditioned notion of "significant issues" we have. The Gospel is ludicrously incongruous in our world. It is *not* headline material. It cannot make it onto the CBS news. If it, or some facsimile of it, does, then it is something other than the Gospel. It may be information, even truthful information, about the activity of the church or certain celebrities who are Christian. But it is not the Gospel.

During the last Holy Week, my eye was caught by an article at the bottom of the page of the Sunday paper. "Prophet Stirs Middle East." Oh no, I thought, not another jerk muddying the waters of world peace. I read on, to have my apprehensions confirmed. "The turbulent Mideast situation is being made even worse by the actions of a self-styled prophet." Oh well, I thought, this sounds like small time stuff. He'll either be assassinated or put in jail before he can do much harm.

I pride myself in not being a gullible person, yet I admit with embarrassment that not till I reached the second paragraph where Jesus was mentioned by name, did I recognize the trick. I attribute my gullibility in this instance to the skillful use of preformulated media language that has become for us an unquestioned vehicle of reality. Phrases such as "presumed confrontation with religious and civil leaders," "turbulent Mideast situation," and "reports indicate that"—precisely because they are heard so often and always in the context of "news," that is, significant reality—led me to accept immediately the story as "real."

And isn't the story real? Well yes, we answer hesitantly. But not real in the same way as the PLO and Menachem Begin are real. Does it strike us, even now, that should anyone read this fifty years hence, they will wonder what those letters stood for and who Begin was, while the "self-styled prophet" of the Middle East will still be around, if only as an artifact?

But did not the people of Jesus' time first hear about him through a mediated source, namely rumors at the town well or the temple gates? Yes. And then they went out to see for themselves. Pharisees and prostitutes, tax collectors and lepers, fishermen and widows. We, however, do not go to see for ourselves. There is no need to. We have others to see for us. We do not experience directly.

The content of the Gospel is inescapably grotesque. That is a recurring scriptural theme. Can the content be accounted foolishness and a stumbling block and the form be culturally camouflaged? At the height of western culture, this central fact of the grotesqueness of the Gospel was not denied. Grunewald's crucifixion painting, for example, which makes us shudder at its gore, was accepted as true by a people who were used to the constant jostling of beauty and ugliness, wealth and poverty, death and life. Perhaps not many actually followed St. Francis' example of embracing the lepers, but at least it made sense to them that a saint should do so. Today it would be dismissed as a silly, senseless gesture. The thing to do would be to get those people to a sanatorium, provide funds for genetic research, invent new and better artificial limbs. That is the kind of charity that makes sense to us.

Our task as a culture has been to eliminate all paradoxes. We have appropriated the sensible moral teaching of the Gospel as our standard of conduct to which we pay public lip service, so much so that we are incensed by a writer like Ayn Rand who strips away the epidermis of ethical pretense. We are also uneasy with an avowedly Christian writer such as Flannery O'Connor who tells us that in her stories "the devil accomplishes a good deal of groundwork that seems to be necessary before grace is effective" (*Mystery and Manners*, p. 117). We should like to rewrite the parables today so that the grain of wheat falling into the ground need not die in order to be born to new life. The prodigal need never go to the far country, the man from Jericho never fall among thieves. It is the hope of our culture to eliminate the need for paradox, for sudden reversal, by instead perfecting the techniques of cloning, effective parenting, and crime prevention.

The sudden change, the jolting, disjunctive nature of paradox we aspire to replace with the steady, smooth upward curve on the development chart. Yes, we say. Our cultural goal is to come out in the end in the same place as the Gospel, with plentiful harvests, happy families, and safe highways. Any segment of "Sixty Minutes" or "Face the Nation" will tell you as much. It is simply that we want to get there by a different route: a sensible, well-organized system of budgeting, planning, and evaluation. Not through some unpredictable, incongruous, uncontrollable force. Nothing as grotesque as the prophets or Nebuchadnezzar or grace. We will accept, we have accepted wholeheartedly, the ends. As a culture we do indeed thirst after justice and righteousness. We are smitten with the specter of starvation and revolted by the advocates of lifeboat ethics. No other culture in the history of the world has had the luxury of such a good conscience. It is only the means we object to, the way God's grace is mediated. The content is great; it's the form we can't abide. It simply won't sell in our culture.

This is not to say that scenes do not appear on our TV sets that, even a few decades ago, would have been considered grotesque. Practically nothing now remains outside the range of the camera. Sex, starvation, murder, madness, Evel Knievel, Jimmy Swaggart, South American pygmies, basketball giants. Literally all sounds and sights, all visual and audible human experience have been appropriated by the camera and recorder. Nothing is too strange, too revolting, too bizarre for us now. By inflating our sensory capacity to incredible limits, we have made all things not only credible but banal. There is no longer any possibility of experiencing the incongruous. All unaware, we have moved into the zoo. Nothing is fantastically extravagant now. Not the mating habits of orangutans or Oklahomans. Not Mars nor Madagascar. Not Idi Amin nor the Ice Capades.

Nothing except three things. These are the grotesque trinity of our culture, the incongruous triad that cannot fit in, the rejected realities. They are silence, hiddenness, and mystery.

The image of an isolated Trappist monastery need not immediately flash into our minds at the introduction of these three words. Secular artists since the nineteenth century have been overwhelmed by the need to reclaim the grotesque, to paint "what is really there" hidden away from our limited vision, to incorporate long, uncomfortable periods of silence into musical compositions or plays, to accumulate syntactically obscure words into poetry which no one can figure out. Silence, hiddenness, and mystery have for almost a century now been the weapons of secular artists. Simultaneously, they have been for the church the stone which has been rejected in the building of media-edifices.

For many ages in human history, the task of the artist has been to gather up the yearnings, the desires, the values of his culture and to give these fragments meaningful shape. The results have been cathedrals, pyramids, tragedies, plainsong. These fortunate—and significantly anonymous—artisans had no need to "forge the uncreated conscience" of their age as James Joyce's young artist resolved to do. They had the somewhat more satisfactory job of creating objects

of contemplation that embodied an already forged understanding of their world.

Despite their youthful exuberances, neither Joyce's
young artist nor any of his successors have achieved anything like that initial goal. Either they did not have the raw
material to forge such a formidable creation, or the world
to which they offered their gift was unimpressed. The result
has been, as Susan Sontag says, that "the artist is continually tempted to sever the dialogue he has with an audience.
Silence is the furthest extension of that reluctance to communicate. . . . Silence is the artist's ultimate other-worldly
gesture: by silence, he frees himself from servile bondage to
the world . . ." (*ibid.*, p. 6).

In maintaining silence, the artist separates himself from
society in as thoroughly effective a way as any Desert Father. For our culture will tolerate any words, any noise—
whether of airplanes or rock bands—but not silence. Even
Punk Rock, initially received in this country with revulsion
and getting its original impetus from an attempt to reclaim
the grotesque, is being defused and emptied of its shocking
content simply by media coverage. (Notice how the meta-
phorically antithetical terms "coverage" and "exposure" have
come to mean the same thing in media terminology.) Punk
rock, reckoned by its originators to be the last outpost of the
grotesque, has been co-opted by the simple technique of de-
sensitizing. Even the Girl Scout national magazine recently
carried an article on "punk chic," the newest clothes fad for
teenage girls. This too now takes its place on the shelf beside
every other communicable variety of human experience in
the supermarket of life-styles.

But not silence. Silence maintains its power to startle
and shock. When confronted with silence our culture reacts
like Brer Rabbit meeting the Tar Baby. We shout at it, strike
out at it, insist upon its answering us. We react with such
violence to silence because we see it, and rightly so, as a
response to our triviality. It is not a mere lag in the con-
versation but a loud indictment, a heaping of coals on our
heads. Is, for instance, the reaction of the churches against
all the bastardized forms of Eastern mysticism purely on

theological grounds or is there not also a reaction to the unspoken accusation made by the expanse of silence incorporated into their spirituality, a silence that has been discarded by the noisy, never-ending "dialogues," the chattering "fellowship," the packaged words on cassette tapes? Indeed, is not silence itself a theological proposition?

The ancient liturgical injunction to "Let all mortal flesh keep silence" is not only ignored but resented. No one is allowed to keep silence, not in group therapy nor press conferences. Instead we are called upon to communicate. All marriages can presumably be saved through communication, children salvaged from ruin if only we can find the right way of putting things. Nations will no longer go to war and denominations will unite if the wording of treaties and resolutions can be worked out, the magic words found and repeated.

Has no one noticed that communication is a matter of sound and communion one of silence?

The secret fear of the Christian church, of course, is that if we ever shut up, no one will pay any attention to us. We are not really so compelled by the Great Commission that we find it impossible not to speak to our neighbors about Christ. In fact, what is called "personal witnessing" is no doubt at an all-time low. Instead, we send contributions to Billy Graham so he can do it for us. And so much more effectively, we explain. Or if we imagine our sensibilities to be more refined, we form and fund a Media Commission at the upper echelons of the church structure to produce clever little radio and TV "spots."

We want our culture to pay attention to the church. We are hurt when its voice is ignored. With the most insufferable self-righteousness we make press releases either for or against homosexuality and Rhodesia. I suspect that the underlying reason for televising evangelistic crusades is to show the rest of the world just how many people such an event can attract—as many as an NFL game. And to reassure ourselves of our reality, which exists only in its plenitude in the public domain. Those of us sitting before our television sets at home, unseen and silent, are somehow submerged beneath the level of full reality. We are hidden from "the public eye" and exist only in potential reality. And what is the public eye but the TV camera? We desperately want that eye, that validating attention, focused on us, on what we profess to believe in. It is more important, more demonstratively efficacious, than the eye of God.

"In one of its aspects," Sontag remarks, "art is a technique for focusing attention, for teaching skills of attention." I took drawing lessons for a time from an artist friend. I began to suffer from such severe vertigo that I had to quit. The world began to swell around me with such advancing and retreating detail that the very earth seemed to heave as soon as I opened my eyes on it. The paradisal state of Adam and Eve, wandering creation in wonder, grew newly significant. There would be enough human work to fill forever just looking.

Art, by drawing out, emphasizing, juxtaposing, forces our attention. I once went through a whole year of seeing the world in terms of Andrew Wyeth. Vision concentrated itself into rusted curves of the earth and shadowy interiors and faces whose lives were on them. How is this different from pictures perceived on a TV screen? Can it too not teach us to focus our attention?

Not so long as it distracts. Not so long as the whole context in which it exists is distraction—from anxiety, from boredom, from isolation. By this I do not mean distraction as opposed to useful instruction, but distraction as opposed simply to attention. Whereas, for example, the attention engendered in art lessons left me with a sense of the world being too wide and wonderful for my sensory circuitry ever to fully comprehend, the same amount of time spent watching television produces jadedness, nausea, and restlessness. That is the effect of distraction as opposed to attention. Network television is intended to distract, the news programs no less than Carol Burnett.

This is no polemic about how television should stop wasting its time with distractions and get down to the serious business of teaching us all Esperanto and healthy nutrition. It is simply an investigation of how, or if, the Gospel can actually fit into the current context of television.

First of all, consider the physical circumstances of the television set in your living room, den, or bedroom. See the entire room, the chairs, the tables, the windows, the floor, and walls. Now take a mental razor blade and cut a small hole along one wall, one certainly no bigger than one-sixtieth of the average wall space. That hole is in, but not of, the room. At any time you can get up, go to the refrigerator, answer the door, turn up the thermostat, use the bathroom, paint your fingernails, comment on the program to your companion, pick up your knitting. All this is in contrast, say, to the movies where the whole intent of the context is to absorb your total attention. The theater is necessarily dark, blotting out surrounding distractions, and the screen is large, larger than your entire living room wall. The difference is important.

That is only the spatial context. Now consider the chronological context. Preceding the attempted presentation of the Gospel is, perhaps, "Match Game P.M." Following it is "How the West Was Won." And, of course, bracketing those are several commercials. McDonald's hamburgers, Midas mufflers, and Fresca. Into this setting of *divertissement* and marketing comes the Gospel. Incongruous enough, we would all agree. Certainly the values and the underlying assumptions of the Way, the Truth, and the Life will be so starkly juxtaposed with concupiscence, violence, and materialism that it will immediately blaze out, dazzling the bored viewer.

Does this happen? Is the figure stretched out in the recliner immediately struck in the solar plexus by the power of this unexpectedly good news? Unfortunately, no. Indeed, it may take him a while to catch on to the fact that this is a "religious" program unless he has checked the *TV Guide* first, in which case he has avoided the experience altogether. There is singing and a little choreography. Spotlights, sets, pretty girls, sporty fellows, all grinning from ear to ear. Then come the guitars, the hand-held mikes, the easy swivel chairs, and coffee tables. And the commercials: the complimentary copy of a paperback book that will change your life and the apologetic, elliptical appeals for broadcasting money.

No, the Gospel in this context is not incongruous at all. In fact, every attempt possible is made to disguise whatever lingering out-of-placeness may cling to it. The point indeed is to integrate every TV cliché, every technique of distraction, so that it will seem to fit and people will not flick the channel knob in disgust. Which they do anyway. The Oral Roberts special, despite the expensive technology available to its producer, is still on a par with Lawrence Welk.

The productions of the liberal wing of the church fare no better. They have simply chosen another set of television clichés to emulate, usually a "serious" talk show or a PBS documentary. They discuss how the audience may develop its human potential or how the social sciences are contributing to our understanding of the religious impulse. They strive to avoid the very appearance of entertainment, and by and large they succeed. The result is even drearier than the aging Pat Boone. Still, it is primarily a distraction, in this case from the particularity of life to the abstractions about it, the "important issues."

Yet every suggestion that Christians abandon the airwaves to the heathens is shouted down. What if the Texans of Southern Baptist persuasion had bought radio and TV spots and instead of Eldridge Cleaver and the yo-yo champion had presented thirty full seconds of silence and a blank screen? What if Sunday morning programming brought nothing but a vast wasteland, a veritable howling desert of silence? What if the distraction was removed? The hole in the living room wall a blank dead space instead of filled with flickering images? What if, one weekday evening, the entire prime time was empty, silent, all across America, bought up and cancelled by the National Council of Churches? The repercussions are too terrifying to contemplate. Churches would be burned to the ground, the national guard called out, conspiracies uncovered. The opium of the people would have been ruthlessly ripped from them and they would react with the violence of a deprived addict.

Should we then, at this time when the screens go dead all over the country, ring our neighbor's doorbell to evangelize him in the flesh? "No indeed," answers Walker Percy, "for in these times everyone is an apostle of sorts, ringing doorbells and bidding his neighbor to believe this and do that. In such times, when everyone is saying 'Come!' when radio and television say nothing else but 'Come!' it may be that the best way to say 'Come!' is to remain silent. Sometimes silence itself is a 'Come!' " (*ibid.*, p. 148).

Silence is the only way of either getting or focusing attention today. All else is a distraction. Yet silence is the great grotesquerie and distraction is the norm.

All that can be said of silence can also be said of hiddenness. It goes against the grain of a neurologically extended culture to have anything hidden from it. All experience must be exposed to the groping tentacles of the network of nerve endings. And all wishes to be exposed, as far as the sensory network extends, unconfined by primitive notions of locality. A central fact shared by all religions, pagan, Christian, and heretical, has been forgotten by their twentieth-century inheritors: hiddenness is the necessary habitat of religious truth. Elaborate initiation rites have always hedged in the elusive truths from the approach of the unworthy. The American Indians guarded the Ghost Dance from photographers. Purification is necessary for admittance to Moslem temples. Even Zen Buddhists protect precious truths by camouflaging them in seemingly pointless koans.

During Augustine's time the sanctuary was cleared before the celebration of the eucharist, and baptized members were forbidden to reveal the secrets of that special communion either to pagans or catechumens. All these we attribute to some primitive, magical instinct, never questioning our own universal obliteration of the secluded and private. Even that area once called our "private lives" is no longer really private. Disclosures once confined to confessionals or bedrooms are now forced upon group participants of one kind or another.

Yet we are told that our "life is hid with Christ in God." We have taken the injunction to let our light shine before men to mean getting prime time coverage. But what about the parable comparing the Kingdom of God to the leaven that was hidden in three measures of meal? Has intimate truth been entirely eaten up by public knowledge?

The former concept scarcely even makes sense to us any longer. Why, after all, should anyone want to hide anything? If a person has any exceptional degree of skill, understanding, beauty, or money, he or she must be interviewed by *People* magazine. None of those qualities can actually be doled out to the rest of us, but the perception of them, the vicarious savoring provided through our culture's extended sensory mechanisms, not only can but must be made available to all. To kccp them to oneself is actually a violation of contemporary moral codes.

We see a further manifestation of this phenomenon of privacy being consumed by publicity in the current trends in psychology. The early preoccupation with psychoanalysis, a situation involving only two people, one of whom is charged with keeping the secrets of the other, has fallen before the insistent "sharing" of group therapy, where, like a potluck supper, everyone must contribute some morsel and no one is allowed to keep anything back for himself.

An interviewer asks a President about his sleeping arrangements with his wife. The amazing thing is that the President answers instead of ordering the interviewer off the premises.

Rock stars never receive so much criticism as when they withdraw from public view. Multitudes of articles were published following Bob Dylan's and Paul McCartney's retreat into seclusion, all of them written with the accusing tone of the rejected lover. It is reprehensible, they all without exception cried, to become famous and then to deprive the media of the exploitation of its own creation. That's biting the hand that feeds you!

But there must have been a reason why Jesus himself

insisted on no publicity. Why did he adjure his followers, after their recognition of him as Messiah, to tell no one? The very concept eludes us today, just as we wonder what the point of guarding the sacrament from the uninitiated was. Every impulse of our culture is aimed at the opposite direction, at exposure and coverage. When Malcolm Muggeridge dared to suggest that Jesus, coming in our time, would turn down free time on television and would indeed consider such an offer a fourth temptation of the devil, his audience was incensed. The idea was unthinkable. Hiddenness strikes us not only as grotesque but as nonsensical.

But beyond the silence and hiddenness lies mystery, which transcends them both and is therefore infinitely more despised than they are by our culture. To a society that has staked its spirituality on *scientia* rather than *sapientia*, knowledge instead of wisdom, mystery must remain the enemy. The society is confident, however, for mystery is a passive enemy; it only sits there, waiting to be exterminated by the accretion of facts. Mystery is ultimately doomed, we think. Given enough time and money, our technology will reveal all secrets, from the farthest quasar to the nearest sub-atomic particle. The very notion that there is something, anything, that by its very nature *cannot* be known to us inside the prison of our five senses, whips us into a fury.

Quoting Sontag again: "Whatever is wholly mysterious is at once both psychically relieving and anxiety-provoking" (*ibid.*, p. 29). That is, in mystery we recognize not nonsense but a truth, something more solid than ourselves. We are comforted that there is something stronger than the mere appearances around us. But at the same time, as creatures of our culture, we are goaded by the irritating realization that the truth concealed in the mystery is beyond our comprehension. What we want is "to take it all in," rather than "to be taken in"; a position we try to avoid at all costs. It is as though we are shouting to God, "All right, come out. We know you're there!" And when all we see is a ripple on the surface or an echo of laughter, we grow furious and refuse to play any longer.

Mystery, it hardly needs to be pointed out, is not suitable material for the media. At their highest pitch of honesty and integrity, the electronic media can only attempt to reproduce as accurately as possible the visible and audible world. They "clone" the surface of reality.

Now should anyone suggest that there is anything beneath the surface, any protoplasm of reality that the membrane of the visible is only just holding back, they are categorized by the cultural mainstream as cultists. It makes no difference to this culture whether such believers belong to Krishna or Christ. All those outside the orthodoxy of scientific spirituality are cultists, diagnosed either as escapists or primitives.

Yet the New Testament never uses the term mystery except with awe and reverence. It is, by Paul's definition, what "eye hath not seen, nor ear heard." It comprises the "deep things of God" which the Spirit itself must search out. Yet, miraculously, it is given to God's people to "speak the wisdom of God in a mystery, even the hidden wisdom, which God ordained before the world unto our glory."

I asked a minister recently if he considered himself a "steward of the mysteries of God," another Pauline description. He looked at me in shock and dismay, assuring me that, on the contrary, he was a "facilitator." There was nothing mysterious to him about the Christian faith. It was as though I had said something obscene. He perceived of himself as dealing with information rather than secrets.

In an age that feeds on data—gathering, storing, and retrieval—secrets are not only grotesque but odious. We scoff at the Transcendental Meditation people who pay a high price for their secret mantras. Well and good, except that our ridicule is for the wrong reason. We have discarded the very concept of a "word of power," whether it be a mantra or the undisclosed secret name given to Navaho tribal initiates. Data are indiscriminately available information. Secrets are their antithesis. Information is an unquestioned and universally accepted value in our culture. Therefore, mystery is an empty category for us. We simply don't see the point of it.

At the moment of the crucifixion, according to Matthew, the temple veil was torn in two, a theme elaborated upon by the author of Hebrews who saw the event as the initiation of the new era, the priesthood of all believers. This did not mean, however, that the camera rolled into the holy of holies, documenting its contents like the tomb of Tutankhamen. Christ himself has become the high priest, mediating the grace of God, the final mystery, directly to our hearts.

It is indeed mediation that is the central issue here. How does what we have come to call "the media" relate to the one we know as the mediator? Are the media, as is being claimed, neutral in themselves, or is there something in their very nature, their electronic extension, their publicness, their distancing from the source, their standing between us and reality—even the reality of flesh and blood, much less the spirit—that perverts our reception of grace? Are the media, with their ultimate linking up of the world's neurological system, the new tower of Babel, not vertically erected this time, but thrown like a net over the earth? I suppose the builders of the tower claimed moral neutrality for their structure, just as advocates of electronic media make the same claim today. Yet both the tower and the net alter the allegiance of the imagination, the very perception of reality. They give the illusion of access to God, or in the absence of God, to ultimate reality.

Anything can be used by God to accomplish his purposes, the media apologists say. Yet the tower of Babel was not refurbished as a high rise office building nor even a temple to the Most High. It was left deserted and decaying.

There is another part of the Babel story that is instructive. The tower-builders' purpose was to "make a name for themselves," lest they be "scattered abroad upon the face of the whole earth." It seems to me that Christians are obsessed with the same motive. Having already been scattered abroad by their Lord's command (although not always by their obedience to that command), they are now determined to make a name for themelves. How much finer a satellite in the sky than a mere terrestrial tower! How much more comfortable to have our task of pilgrimage and sojourn re-

solved by electronic evangelism. We write a check and stretch
out in the recliner to hear the experts present the message
we are financing, absolved of the arduous task of intimate
human contact. After all, we may sweat and stammer if we
have to bear our own witness. And what are two or three
gathered together when we can have two or three million?

Yet if we can no longer even see the Grand Canyon
because of the barrier of the media package, how can we
possibly see Jesus through all the media hype?

Almost a century ago, Nietzsche called for a "transval-
uation of values." It was the method in his madness that
was accurate, if not the content. We have, in fact, despite
ourselves, adopted the values of the Superman, if indeed the
world had ever abandoned them. Christians must always be
transvaluing the cultural values that surround them. If we
think the Kingdom is upon us, via satellite and transistors,
we are mistaken. The media do not record, are not even
interested in, the still, small voice. What eye hath not seen
nor ear heard is antithetical to its existence.

The Gospel, in whatever age if finds itself, is always out
of place, incongruous, extravagant, not pretty, unpackage-
able, unmanageable, grotesque. In this age, that means silence, hiddenness, and mystery. If we want to make a name
for ourselves, we will have to go somewhere besides the
Gospel.

Anything can be used by God to accomplish his purposes, the media apologists say. This is the rationale used
most often by what we have come to call the "mainline denominations." (This is itself a media phrase created to make
easy but not always accurate distinctions.) Even Roman
Catholics (and who more mainline than they?) have recently
begun to bemoan the fact that ever since Bishop Fulton J.
Sheen faded from the screen in 1957, their church's media
image has been overshadowed by Protestant superstars. Pope
Paul VI made an effort in 1975 to reestablish a claim to
mass media through his "Evangelii Nuntiandi" message.
The quaint irony of exhorting the use of electronic media in
a Latin treatise possibly escaped him. At any rate, the
American bishops came up with the idea of taking a special

national collection for breaking into media—or "communications." The plan was attacked by the Catholic Press Association, however, because they felt the term "communications" was misleading. Contributors might think they were subsidizing their favorite religious periodical when actually most of the hoped-for $7 million was to go to electronic media to vindicate the television ghost of Bishop Sheen. Although the CPA was eventually placated and the Catholic Communications Campaign was waged, the questions of how the money will be spent are still unresolved.

Seven million dollars is peanuts in electronic media. Despite its large membership, the church has not produced a successor to Sheen. Therefore, should they go with thirty-second spots like the Texas Southern Baptists and the Mormons? Microwave networks? Instructional material? More Paulist films? The bishops with their seven million are in the position of four-year-olds with a nickel in the candy store. The choice is limitless. The money is minuscule. Yet the question of whether the collection was a good idea or not was raised only by segments of the Catholic press, and then only for survival motives.

Ellwood Keiser, president of Paulist Productions, made a plea for his church's media collection in the Jesuit magazine, *America*: "Ours is a media culture. Increasingly, *for better or worse*, electronic media, particularly television, have become dominant. Television has created a new set of symbols by which we think and new role models from which to choose" (May 6, 1978, p. 559, italics mine). Why has the import of the phrase "for better or worse" been ignored? If electronic media are indeed *for worse*, why should millions of Roman Catholic faithful be asked to contribute to it? What are the new symbols and the new role models television has presented us with? Kojak? Charlie's Angels? The Oakland Raiders? It is neither the symbols nor the role models that are new with television. They are the same old ones based on power, violence, and sexual exploitation that the world has always known. What is new about electronic media is their mass alienation of a whole culture through its altered perceptions of reality.

Actually, Roman Catholics should be grateful that the proposed "national media strategy" is so out of touch with what television is really about. Their seven million dollars is unlikely to do any real harm. It reflects, in fact, the usual fuzzy understanding that most mainline denominations have about media. Such items as establishing a research institute to study the impact of electronic evangelism, Television Awareness Training workshops, lobbying the FCC, funding diocesan media offices—all these will have as much impact, for better or worse, on our media culture as perhaps the PTA.

The collection and the strategy show the same unquestioning acceptance of the nature of mass media and the same lack of understanding as the 191st General Assembly of the United Presbyterians. Their "mission rationale" statement for such involvement began thus: "The United Presbyterian Church ought to be involved in mass media" (*The General Assembly Daily News*, May, 1979, p. 12). The closest the document comes to rationally substantiating this dogma, however, is to appeal to the fact that everyone, both the churched and the unchurched, owns television sets. It also makes the obvious point that the media "directly influences social mores." By what means and to what good end remains unspecified. The unexamined presuppositions of the paper take a more sinister turn, however, when it claims that "understanding and commitment on the part of church members is a function of information." If all we need are facts, why do so many United Presbyterians remain untouched by the deluge provided by their Interpretation and Stewardship committees? Can they really not read? Or hear? Have they indeed fallen asleep during those boring after-dinner filmstrips? If information is all we need, what becomes of inspiration? Presbyterians are canny on one point, though. The paper calls mass media "a powerful tool" for increasing the giving of church members. This is indeed the "new set of symbols" television has given us. It's called "commercials."

Again, fortunately, in typical mainline fashion, the Presbyterians are out of step and will remain ineffective with media. While PTL puts up a satellite, the General Assembly voted to continue the mass media task force for another year. This is the unswerving mainline reaction to befuddlement. At the end of a year, the task force is to make a report recommending a "program design" for media. It will no doubt look very like the Catholic bishop's "strategy." It will be largely taken up with lecturing the public on the dangers of sex, violence, and sugar-coated cereal on television with a plea for more minorities and women to portray "powerful" roles. It will reflect the sort of thinking in the articles on media by secretary for communications at the National Council of Churches, William Fore (*viz.* "Mass Media's Mythic World: At Odds with Christian Values," *Christian Century*, January 19, 1977). It will no doubt provoke a big yawn from audiences everywhere.

James A. Taylor, managing editor of the *United Church Observer* and former worker in radio and television, is a voice crying in the mainline wilderness. He probes past the superficial problems of media to study their essential nature. "Jesus," he says, "would have been safe as a TV star—protected by public relations staffs, the technology of bright lights and zoom lenses, and audiences that applaud on cue. . . . People, you see, can be vulnerable. But the mass media can never be. . . . In print the New Journalism indulges in a lot of first-person narrative, as I have done in this article— as if I were really laying myself open to your criticisms. But I'm not. By the time you can respond, I will have gone on to something entirely different." It is the immediacy of personal presence, which carries with it the risk of rejection that Taylor sees as the essence of evangelism. "I think that if Jesus had had TV, if Paul had had a printing press, Christianity might never have survived," he claims. "The early Christians would have been tempted to leave the job of evangelism to the communications experts" (*Christian Century*, May 30, 1979, p. 614).

Chapter V:

THE PEOPLE'S WORK

"TV is very mysterious unless you are in it all the time. Then it gets to be another piece of equipment. You don't think about the consequences of what you are doing. . . . The camera becomes a friend."—Pat Robertson

AN IMPORTANT PART OF the strategy in our current culture's attempt to reinvent its spirituality has been to attack the church and its worship as subversive. What is called "organized religion" is fundamentally at odds with the supposedly spontaneous spirituality of our time. Whatever forces planned the strategy, they were indeed diabolically clever, for they recruited the leaders of the church itself to actually carry out the attack.

The plan unfolded something like this. 1) The church's manner of worship is dull and outmoded. It no longer appeals to "modern man." 2) The church must continue to grow and change (key words in contemporary value systems) in order to relate meaningfully to this modern man. 3) Our patterns of worship must therefore be refurbished and made more appealing. 4) The pattern for remodelling that we should follow is what is now most appealing to the majority of modern men.

With such reasoning, it is little wonder that the result of the refurbishing looked like a grand opening at the supermarket. There was guitar-playing, folk singing, dancing in the aisles, all in a self-conscious attempt to "celebrate," which was the updated word for worship. There were dialogues rather than sermons. Also skits, clowns, balloons, and puppet shows.

No one went about the task of breaking out of the tight dead skin of liturgical patterns and emerging into new, revivified forms by a jubilant rediscovery of these same elements in the traditions of the church. Neither the medieval cycle plays nor Hebrew and Shaker dancing were studied as paradigms. The fervid, fourth-century congregations whose enthusiasm surpassed even the wildest dreams of Harvey Cox were never held up as examples of participatory worship. All the things that liturgical innovators have tried in order to attract that elusive phantasm, modern man, have been done before in the church's worship, and done much better.

What came of all this considerable effort was instead a pale imitation of a "media event." Marlo Thomas' television special "Free to Be You and Me" was translated into church education curriculum programs. Regional assemblies of church bodies were treated to, or assaulted by, according to one's orientation, ever grander extravaganzas of mediocrity.

Still, nothing happened. In the competition for the titillation, stimulation, and entertainment of human sensibilities, the church came in somewhere behind the travelling carnival in the supermarket parking lot. Somehow the promised patrons did not materialize. Modern man was neither amused nor impressed. The church, with its limited resources of money and talent, failed miserably in the production of media events.

For one thing, the essential ingredient in a media event was missing. Namely the cameras and recorders and cables. Some of the more clever ones among us were able to catch on to this eventually. They went the one essential step farther and instead of simply staging a homemade, locally limited "celebration," they introduced the element of broadcasting. Film and tape are manipulatable media. They can be spliced, edited, voiced over, polished. Real professionals can be enlisted to enact the celebration. The product is predictably slicker than the neighborhood choir and a small-time pastor. Guest stars, Christian celebrities—that's what will work.

Did anyone point out that there is no such thing as a Radio Church, that theologically it is a contradiction in terms? In our rush to support modern man's spirituality in the style to which he had become accustomed, we had forgotten the one thing necessary for worship—total presence. Even supposing that it were possible for an evangelistic crusade to be efficacious as a mediated event, worship requires immediacy, being there. There are very few human experiences where one must still be physically present to participate in them, so far has technology extended our nerve-endings. Birth and death, sex and liturgy, remain the hold-outs. None of these can be performed satisfactorily by proxy or long distance.

It is no wonder, then, that media religion has developed both an anti-church basis and an anti-church bias, or that it flagrantly competes for the Christian ecclesiastical dollar. As the little puppet on the PTL Club so crassly put it, "Being spiritual is not just going to church and putting your money in the offering plate." No indeed. But pledging $100 to The Total Image Center is getting close.

Media productions are universally valued by our culture and consequently their cost is high. Satellites don't grow on trees. Marriott conference rooms cost money. Billboards are not free. Telephone switchboards are expensive. Television spots are the pearl of astronomically great price. Somebody has got to pay for all that exposure. To the media religious leaders every dollar saved from the offering plate is a dollar earned for the next blitz.

Yet in this unacknowledged battle between "organized" and media religion, the church has one great secret weapon. Media religion may be flashier, but worship can only take place in the gathered body of Christ. The pastor and the congregation must be present to one another, physically as well as spiritually. In the Lord's supper, in baptism, in ordination, people actually have to touch one another. A radio church cannot administer sacraments.

Liturgy, the form that corporate worship takes, means literally, the people's work. That work, whether undertaken in a red-neck Pentecostal service or in the most elevated high-church eucharist, consists of lifting up the heart. Sometimes it seems that a construction crane is required to accomplish the task. At other times the merest touch will suffice to levitate it. But that remains the work of the people, and it cannot be done alone. The worship leader, whether priest or lay-preacher, acts as the quirt, rallying the hearts for the effort required of them. And precisely because the effort is so considerable, every ounce of energy and encouragement is needed. No matter how awful the joyful noise they make, the singers that surround one on Sunday generate a spiritual energy that comes from a dimension inaccessible to the most sophisticated technology.

It doesn't take many to make a congregation. Two or three will do. But it is necessary for them to be gathered together for Christ to be in the midst of them. Time and space are the limitations he has imposed. They are the very ones the media, indeed our whole culture, seeks to destroy.

Our culture has tried to storm heaven and become eternal by technologically transcending time and space. Yet we are once again up against a paradox. One must enter eternity, it seems, through submitting to time and space. Universality is achieved only through stubborn insistence on locality. "Men esteem truth remote," Thoreau wrote in *Walden*, "in the outskirts of the system, behind the farthest star, before Adam and after the last man. In eternity there is something true and sublime. But all these times and places and occasions are now and here. . . . And we are enabled to apprehend what is sublime and noble, only by the perpetual instilling and drenching of the reality that surrounds us."

Bryan Wilson, an Oxford sociologist, explains how much religion is at odds with the basic structures of contemporary culture: "religion is always primarily a communal, as distinct from a societal, institution. Its operation is always essentially local. The basic commodity that religion purveys—reassurance about salvation—must be available wherever its agents operate. The vital activities to reassure men must be replicated over time and space. . . . Every local agent must have adequate competence as a purveyor of the commodity with which the Church is concerned" (*Contemporary Transformations of Religion*, Oxford University Press, 1976, pp. 89-90).

In other words, if there is not an actual functioning church in any given human community, then the church, literally, *is not there*, no matter how many religious programs are beamed into that neighborhood daily.

Advertisements for the Red Cross or the United Way often tell us that "we are there" at the site of disasters or deprivation through the money that we contribute to relief efforts. But money also is only a medium. We are not really there. This is a very basic but necessary distinction, one that is difficult for us to get a firm grip on since we have become so accustomed to living a mediated life. After a while we begin to believe what we hear. We forget where we are. We become disoriented from the brute reality of time and space. "That's the way it is," Walter Cronkite tells us, "today, May 2, 1978." And we believe that we have lived the same May 2 as has just flashed before our eyes. We become abstracted out of our own lives—the work we have done that day, the promises we have made or broken, the landscape we have inhabited, the people we bump up against— and instead haunt like ghosts the "world life" of mediated experience. We dream that we have transcended time and space.

As we are skewered by the human condition to one limited locale, however, we are also caught in the coordinates of time. Again, this puts us at odds with the pressures of rapidization that are an unquestioned value in our society. Bryan Wilson points out that our

> demand to see religion "working," engendering emotions, making men do things ... reflects the emphasis in contemporary sales techniques. The old idea of learning, of a steady habilitation, of socialization, of necessarily recurrent dedication to God, "each returning day," is set aside for religion by rapid results. ... The idea of steady growth in grace, perhaps of a lifelong cultivation of understanding, is replaced by the modern demand for instant access to authentic reality. The authenticity is guaranteed by subjective feeling. ... Feeling is quick: but spiritual and intellectual cultures are slow. (*ibid.*, pp. 86-87)

An ordained friend of mine, a leader in the development of "conference ministry," tells me that he believes the parish ministry is on its way out, has been superseded by historical forces to which we would be wise to acquiesce. People no longer actually live in their own homes, with their own families, in their own local neighborhoods. They live in a framework that transcends time and space. They live in the Archie Bunker family or the *Psychology Today* quasi-family. They live in the house on the other side of the looking glass, the soap opera house. Barbara Walters and Jimmy Carter and the Osmonds are their neighbors. They live in the anonymity of mobility and mediation.

Conference ministry caters to this apparition of reality. A husband and wife go off for a weekend to a retreat center where they form a "community" with perhaps a dozen other couples. They get understandably high on the intensity of the encounter, a multiple spiritual affair. What would otherwise be years of knowledge about one another must be abstracted from their pasts and packed into a few short hours, just as in a sexual liaison the feeling is more intense because the years of cohabitation are concentrated into brief interludes. All this takes place, of course, on what is properly termed "neutral territory," the assumption being that locality, place, is extraneous to being. *Who* one is has nothing to do with *where* one is. The couple goes home, elevated by the spiritual affair. If they know they will inevitably come down off the high, they also know there will be a wide selection of religious conferences to choose from next spring. There is no need to have recourse to the local church, which bores them because the faces as well as the hymns are likely to be familiar.

By such attractive addictions the local church is effectively undercut. The result is a kind of playschool religion where the work of the people, the exertion of lifting up their hearts, is replaced by genial exercises in relaxation.

The limitations of locality are outmoded in our culture. And with all the para-church organizations systematically cutting the congregational throat in a friendly gesture of euthanasia, it will indeed be miraculous if the local church survives the century. The sustained existence of the church has always been by miracle, however. To Augustine, dying while Hippo was under siege by the barbarians, the future no doubt looked bleak too. It will prove interesting to see how the Almighty pulls this one off. No doubt our civilization appears as invulnerable to us as the Roman state did to Augustine and Jerome.

At bottom it is everydayness that we scheme to escape by technologically transcending locality. (And getting in a car or plane to travel to "neutral" territory is as much a technological escape as turning a TV dial.) The ordinary is our enemy. Those familiar faces that can never equal the beautiful people on the screen, the unvarying landscape out the kitchen window that never dissolves into the Mediterranean or Capitol Hill, the routine alarm clock and work schedule—it is these that make us despair of our lot in life. How fitting that the largest producers of television sets are Japanese workers who live in company-owned concrete warrens and exercise themselves regularly at mandatory calisthenics. They, more than most, know the value of the magic boxes they make.

One can escape the dissatisfaction with one's life in one of two ways. The most obvious is novelty, either immediate or mediated. One can take up rock-climbing or watch others do it on Wide World of Sports. One can become the leader of a Satanic cult like Charles Manson or read *Helter-Skelter*. The immediate pursuit of novelty, however, is by its very nature full of risks. And to a certain extent it puts one outside his culture, which is one of mediated experience.

Novelty is what the liturgical innovators of recent years have been after. Harvey Cox's description of an Easter celebration he organized in Boston several years ago demonstrates this. Held in a discotheque, it featured remnants of a Byzantine Mass, ritual dances, a light show, body painting, Hindu chanting, and tinsel crowns. Such circus managers are not totally wrong when they announce that the worship in churches is boring and stuck in a rut. But their solution to that ordinariness is novelty. And one can only go on turning so many bends in the road before one comes back home again.

Which brings us to the second alternative. G. K. Chesterton has observed that if you really want to learn about life, the thing to do is stay home. There in the prison of

personalities you will discover more than you ever wanted
to know about human nature, about "life." It is the one who
goes off wandering, who easily disengages himself from un-
pleasant situations, who only skims the surface of life.

It sometimes happens that by memorizing the faces,
learning the landscape, we paradoxically are freed from the
everydayness of our lives. As with Proust tasting his tea
cake, the past comes flooding back upon us, heady with as-
sociations that open as wide as the world. Ordinary water
suddenly turns to wine. How different from Harvey Cox's
desperate novelty is Annie Dillard's backwater worship.
"There is one church here, so I go to it. On Sunday mornings
I quit the house and wander down the hill to the white frame
church in the firs. On a big Sunday there might be twenty
of us there; often I am the only person under sixty, and feel
as though I'm on an archaeological tour of Soviet Russia.
The members are of mixed denominations; the minister is
a Congregationalist, and wears a white shirt. The man knows
God" (*Holy the Firm*, p. 57).

There is nothing, so far as I can see, in our culture that
encourages this recovery of our lives. The impetus is all in
the direction of the other option. Novelty and its corollary,
disposability, is the norm in everything from human rela-
tionships to diapers.

Though the mechanics involved in hoisting the hearts
may vary from age to age, the work of the people in worship
does not change. It is outside chronology. The same psalms
sung four thousand years ago still serve as vessels in which
we raise our complaints and thanksgivings. The chief end
of man is still to glorify God, despite his current designation
as a consumer.

Our lust for transcendence of time and space is not in
error. That has always been one of the truest desires of the
human heart. It is only another way of recognizing death as
our enemy. It was not the impulse to enter heaven that was
the downfall of the tower-builders of Babel, only their way
of getting there. We ourselves are simply setting to work on
the task of transcendence with the wrong tools.

It is not storage technology that will satisfy that desire,

not tape spindles or film cannisters. It is eternal life we crave, not reruns. Nor do we want simply to flush away the life we now lead, disposing of it to make room for the newest style in lives. It is liturgy that makes this possible, that reveals to us our own eternity fulfilled, if only for such a fleet second that we are never sure afterwards that it actually happened. And so have to be periodically reassured.

Eternity is the fruit of time. When we come before God, whether in Sunday morning worship or at the last judgment, we bring with us all that we are. This time, we really are there, in pure immediacy. "God himself is with us," the choir sings. That in itself creates eternity. The communion of saints, both visible and invisible, the gathered body of Christ, is held for a moment in eternal existence. It participates already in the not-yet of the Kingdom. Its worship is a hole in time through which this everyday is funneled into a dimension we cannot yet dream of.

That is why we go back, week after week. It is not novelty we seek when we go; it is repetition of the addictive experience of eternity. Did he *really* say that, we wonder, waiting to be reassured, hoping for the *déja vu* of salvation.

Chapter VI:

THE DANGERS OF
THE DISEMBODIED

"Of reasonable soul and human flesh subsisting."—
Book of Common Prayer

W E NEED TO RETURN at this point to the basic problem with which we began—the frustration of Christians trying to live in a secular society whose entire culture is more and more created, controlled, and communicated by centralized media rather than by communal or local forces. That media have changed our very manner of perceiving the world is unquestioned. Needless to say, when perceptions are changed, so are the values based on those modified perceptions.

We have spent rather a long time describing the disorienting effect this shift to centralized, sensorily remote communication has had on the Christian presence. Both churches and para-ecclesiastical groups have sought to create (the latter more successfully) a satellite Christian culture tricked out in all the trappings of its secular counterpart in the evangelistic hope of making the Christian image, and therefore the Christian message, more appealing.

In the last chapter the fundamental conflict between mediated experience and worship, which requires total *immediate* presence, was explored. This conflict has caused much bewilderment to churches, who have seen the enormous success in the marketplace of the manipulation of the minds and wills of the world's population by media, yet who have failed in their own attempts to capitalize on the power of these magic machines.

But now we must also consider, laying our liturgical lives aside for the moment, if that public, anonymous presence called media can in any way be a tool for implementing the Kingdom of God. Is the phenomenon of media itself neutral, as the opponents of Muggeridge claim, or will it be, like the sword of Charlemagne, judged hereafter as an unfit instrument of God's peace? Is there anything worse than poor taste that appalls us about Christian Johnny Carson shows? Are we only concerned with the quality of Christian media or is there something inherent in the nature of the beast that is antithetical to the spirit of Christ? If the retreat into Christian ghettos turns out to be a historical necessity, as it has been at times in the past, should that ghetto look like a microcosm of the larger society from which it has cut itself off?

We need to remind ourselves again, just to avoid being led down side roads by false questions, that we are not concerned here with the *content* of secular media. We should not, and do not in our clearer-headed moments, expect magazine ads for automobiles and liquor or television shows based on lust to be put together by and for dedicated Christians. We are wasting our time if we expect Christian behavior from a non-Christian world. Rather we are concerned with the nature of media itself, whatever its content, and whether that nature is such that it can be "baptized" and made a faithful servant of the Kingdom. For this response to culture there are certainly many historical precedents. In the ancient world, the pagan festivals of the Saturnalia and the spring fertility rites were successfully incorporated into the church, giving us the great seasons of Christmas and Easter. Thought patterns of the first century that were essentially Greek rather than Hebrew were used to make Christianity intelligible to many Gentiles. But the gladiatorial games were brought to an end, even in the pluralistic society of the Roman Empire, through the agency of Christian martyrs. Augustine waged spiritual war against the north African practice of placating the dead by leaving offerings on graves. Not all cultural quirks can be infused with a new spirit friendly to mankind. Some are so destructive that they must be abjured altogether by Christians. "It is a fallacy of our time," protests Muggeridge, "that we can usefully participate in whatever exists." We need to learn to be at least as discriminating as the ancient church in discerning the spirits that inhabit our own world.

Nevertheless, it is almost impossible not to get bogged down in this quagmire of argument over media. We get distracted by legitimate discussions of sex and violence, whether crime on television elicits crime on the streets. Various denominations make lists of approved secular programs, notable primarily for their inanity, and think they have done their duty in the matter. Agencies of the church give awards to worthy productions with socially redeeming content. Women's groups lobby against commercials for sugar-coated cereal. But these are all beside the point of overt Christian involvement in media. They are all concerned with content rather than the altered perceptions produced by reliance on mediated experience.

I believe Muggeridge's instincts are infallible here. His scenario of Jesus' refusing television coverage of his ministry for the same reasons he refused similar offers of power from Satan is accurate. If he refused to turn stones into bread in order to attract followers, he would refuse also the manipulation of men's minds by media. Yet Muggeridge has not sufficiently satisfied the questioning of those who demand a reason for such extraordinary hypothetical behavior. Perhaps it will be finally futile, this search for a sensible answer. Certainly the disciples, up to the bitter end, expected their Messiah to make use of the materials offered to him by the ruler of this world. To turn stones into bread, to call up legions of angels, or fire down from heaven struck them not only as reasonable but prudent. If military, political, and economic power made sense to them then, what about us now? Do we not ourselves grasp for the proven powerful tools that can make people buy anything, even God? And is not our consternation at our failure with media vaguely reminiscent of the disciples' disgruntled misunderstanding of the Messiah's methods?

Muggeridge's arguments against media are usually based on the dichotomy between reality and fantasy. It is impossible, he says, to tell the truth on television. Here he is a member of a shining company who have always been leery of fiction in whatever form. Plato decided to oust poets from his own idealized Republic because they "told lies." Augustine himself could never get over the fact that the pagan story of Dido moved him to tears even though he knew it to be a fabrication. The sumptuary laws of the Puritan Commonwealth closed the English theaters on the grounds that actors were pretending to be people they were not.

Muggeridge, however, says he does not object to fiction when it is presented as fiction. The reader of a novel, for instance, is aware of the kind of truth or untruth he is dealing with and is responsible for sifting and judging it. Also, there is a name attached to such works so that the reader knows it to be the artifice of a single person. This kind of fiction he opposes to the presentation of "news" which is anonymously selected, edited, telescoped—in short, inescapably manipulated—all in order to show a purported reality.

Mass-disseminated information therefore—and here we are not dealing with intentional fiction—by its very nature demands condensation, simplification, often translation into terms and categories that are understandable to a statistically average audience. Mass media make no sense otherwise. To individualize, amplify, and explore ambiguities means to address a smaller and smaller audience. Supply too many facts, tell too many sides of the story, complicate matters too much and people begin to yawn. Thorough exploration of an issue is antithetical to an industry whose whole existence is based on reaching the largest possible number of people.

Added to this is the fact that the average audience is unconcerned with exactly who prepared the information for their consumption. Nor would it do them any good to attempt to find out. In any case the authorship is conglomerate, just as the audience is, and there is no question of holding any one person responsible for the truth. The information is actually a mosaic made up of the work of many people. We attribute it only corporately to one of the major networks or to some foundation. Besides, do we really watch even the news primarily for its informative value? Is the news content not shaped by the emotional hungers of the audience, serving for us the same purgative purpose theatrical tragedies did for the Greeks?

Then there is the problem of rapidization. The information is here and gone, irretrievable to the ordinary person. Before there is time to consider and digest, here comes another wave of information inundating the audience, demanding attention. This also is the nature of mass media. It saturates, washes the audience, even in printed form. We careen from crisis to crisis. It leaves no space for consideration and contemplation. We feel as though we are on a roller coaster, bombarded by a rush of stimuli we cannot possibly absorb, panicked into paralysis. It does no good for social critics to tell us to take control of our lives, to make thoughtful, reasoned decisions as befits sapient beings. The world is rushing by. Data are being fed into our receptors at an incredible rate. We are told that we must "keep up" with the news, information, what's going on. But we can't. It far outdistances our human capacities to absorb, understand, mull over, decide.

That rapidization by media had already produced altered perceptions in everyone who participates in western civilization, whether or not we consciously choose such modification of our mentality, was noted by Albert Schweitzer from his vantage point in Africa as long ago as 1915: "Newspapers one can hardly bear to look at. The printed string of words, written with a view to the single, quickly-passing day, seems here, where time is, so to say, standing still, positively grotesque. . . . This brings into our general view of life—and this even in the case of the less educated— something which makes us conscious of the feverishness and vanity of the life of Europe. . ." (*The Primeval Forest*, Pyramid, 1963, pp. 112-113). Who knows what Schweitzer would have made of the assault on one's sense of time by electronic media which are invading even his primeval forest today?

But need it be this way in Christian uses of the media, we wonder. Can't we do it better? Can't we change it somehow? I think we need only look to the present boom in religious publishing to see that this has not happened. It is like asking if we might not profit by the mistake of Adam and Eve and so learn better behavior. Books are always assumed to be the most innocuous of all forms of contemporary media. After all, isn't the Bible a book? The proliferation of religious books, however, has come about not because more and better books are being written but because there is a statistically predictable market for them. Cookbooks, diet books, exercise books, sex books, money books, sports books, psychology books. Every element that can be abstracted from secular culture to bolster the Christian culture. We are awash in a sea of supposedly Christian information. Thus have we succeeded in trivializing the infinite.

I recently received an advertisement through the mail for a Christian newsletter that attempts to ferret out and compress this mass of print for me. It purports to be "a capsulized, bi-weekly Kiplinger-type report, prepared in crisp, easy-to-read style that will keep you on top of things." Going on to compare the needs of Christian leaders to those of business executives, it says, "As the world gets more complex and demands on Christian leaders get more intense, *Evangelical Newsletter* meets the specialized news needs of the active Christian quickly, clearly, thoroughly. The editors have pledged themselves to provide the same quality service that Kiplinger provides his secular clientele." The encouragement of the Christian leader to identify himself with the image of a business executive is, of course, obvious. What is even more shocking is the reinforcement of specifically media-related values—condensation and rapidization—values totally and uncritically absorbed into "Christian" media.

The answer to the question "Can't we do it better?" is obviously no. Or at least we haven't. It is the same issue that Jesus dealt with in his camel-through-the-needle's-eye story. None of us wants to believe that it is actually that hard to handle money without being seduced by its power. And no one wants to believe it about media either. Money corrupts not only publicly but privately our best intentions.

Media and their power over information, simplified and speeded to intolerable rates, corrupt our very perceptions, leading us to believe in subtle falsehoods. "Thank you for being with us tonight," says David Brinkley at the end of his newscast. But I haven't been with him at all. I am a thousand miles away with my cat in my lap. The attempt at a false intimacy becomes repugnant once the spell is broken and the reality of time and space reasserts itself. Yet this same attempt at false intimacy is carried to even further extremes in Christian programming.

But isn't *our* information of a different nature from that printed, pictured, and broadcast by secular media? Isn't our content sufficiently strong to overcome the form? When Muggeridge was confronted with the apparent success of his own film documentary on Mother Teresa of India, *Something Beautiful for God*, he admitted that, as Jesus ends the needle's-eye story, nothing is impossible with God. Such a claim for God's power was not meant as a blanket endorsement of getting rich, however. It meant only that, by the grace of God, a rare rich man will, unlike the rich young ruler who provided the occasion for the story, be able to renounce the power of his wealth over him.

Our information is indeed different from that purveyed by the secular media. Our news is Good News. Theirs is almost always bad. It is so bad that it seems inconceivable that people would believe that toothpaste and deodorant, detergent and automobiles will compensate for the televised terrors of this world. By my estimation, Walter Cronkite, as the newsman with the most longevity, ought to be the nation's most confirmed Calvinist, thoroughly convinced of the total depravity of man. Yet the way the network bounces from news catastrophe to comic commercial signifies better than anything else our mediated schizophrenia.

The news we have to tell is no longer so very new now. It has been hanging around history for several centuries. And while we still may believe in the goodness of the Good News, we have lost our faith in its newsworthiness, its power to startle, to surprise, to take off guard. Just as we have been deceived into drawing a facile parallel between Christian leaders and business executives, we have assumed that all information is of the same order and can be communicated in the same ways. But the kind of information we have to share is communal. That fact alone prevents its dissemination through the necessarily falsifying channels of mass media. The Good News requires a knowledge by union; data supplied over distances will not suffice. God with us is not the same as David Brinkley with us.

The secular world in all its sensory extension, its myriad of technical tentacles clutching the globe, is wary of "being taken in." Incredulity is a virtue in our times, and perhaps a necessary one, given the nature of manipulated media reality. We pride ourselves on not being gullible. But it is only by being taken in that we ever understand anything of the life of Christ's body. Incorporation is our only hope of understanding the kind of life that is eternal. As long as we remain separated from God, we can never know him.

Perhaps because sacramental knowledge, even within the church, has been so ignored since the technological age descended on us, we have allowed ourselves to fall into presuppositions about communicating information that severely limit our evangel. Since analytic, scientific modes of thought have been validated as the only way of knowing anything important, and intuitive knowledge that is absorbed as one absorbs the elements has been devalued and discounted as "poetic," meaning impractical, the church has felt uneasy either with mystical language or with its own absurd and inexplicable sacraments. At a recent pastoral installation service, I heard wry clerical jokes about the minister being charged with guarding the mysteries of the sacraments. It was clear that any sort of knowledge that could not be apprehended in a discursive manner was considered of little value. Yet even Calvin, whose chilling intellect is often deplored, was apparently equipped to understand the mysterious working of the sacraments in a way that eludes us. "Even though it seems unbelievable that Christ's flesh, separated from us by such great distance, penetrates to us, so that it becomes our food, let us remember how far the secret power of the Holy Spirit towers above all our senses, and how foolish it is to wish to measure his immeasurableness by our measure. What, then, our mind does not comprehend, let faith conceive: that the Spirit truly unites things separated in space" (*Institutes*, IV, xvii, 10). Here is true intimacy: the Spirit uniting the separated, and without recourse to technology. Notice the imagery of being taken in, of union, as a way of knowing, or rather of conceiving. And mark also Calvin's strangely rapt insistence upon the limits of communicating this knowledge: "And although my mind can think beyond what my tongue can utter, yet even my mind is conquered and overwhelmed by the greatness of the thing. Therefore, nothing remains but to break forth in wonder at this mystery, which plainly neither the mind is able to conceive nor the tongue to express" (*ibid.*, xvii, 7).

There is, of course, such a thing as knowledge *about* God, or at any rate knowledge of our speculation about God. It has a long and venerable tradition within the church. But it is not the same as knowledge *of* God. It is the former kind of knowledge that is indeed easier to communicate. It can in fact be put on cassette tapes. But it is the latter kind of knowledge that "makes disciples." It too must be mediated, but in this case by the Holy Spirit who is a much less predictable and never reproducable power source.

Christians speak earnestly about "meeting individual needs." Then they try to do it by techniques. Any technique, by its very nature, cannot meet *individual* needs which are, by definition, unique. The whole point of technique is to meet mass needs. In the interest of maximum efficiency, it must adjust itself to fit a statistical norm. Techniques are devised to be used over and over again and to eliminate the need for beginning at the first with each new situation. The assumption is that situations are similar enough to make the application of techniques profitable. In physics this is usually true, although even there it has its limits. But one of the many amazing things about the gospels is the absence of technique in Jesus' ministry. There are an extraordinary number of intimate conversations with Jesus recorded and each one is unique. He had a different answer for each seeker. Some he commanded to follow; others he told to go home. Never once did he distribute tracts containing either spiritual laws or plans of salvation. There were, of course, mass gatherings at which he taught about the Kingdom. But, curiously to us for whom efficiency in communication is the first consideration, he adamantly maintained that his audience was incapable of understanding. These mass gatherings, however, were also accompanied by signs—healing and feeding—a means of communication that demands physical proximity. In reading of Christ's ministry on earth we get the sensation of the very life being squeezed out of him as though everyone in the world was trying to get close enough to touch him.

We do not hand our children a book on how to behave when once they learn to read. We know the terrifying truth that they must learn this from living with us, watching us. The means of conveying the information needed to become a human being is necessarily communal. Infants incapable of speech learn their most fundamental and essential information about the universe from the early, inarticulate years. To "know" a person means, if nothing else, to have been in that one's presence, to hear the voice, see the face. If God were only a Principle, an abstraction of certain qualities, then the information about it could indeed be communicated on the same basis and by the same means that we discuss the gold standard or radio isotopes. But there is a difference between knowing data and knowing a person. A person is never reducible to data. God being the Ultimate Person, therefore, knowing him demands ultimate presence, ultimate contact, ultimate communion.

What we don't like about this situation, whether with human beings or with Ultimate Being, is that we cannot control the flow of information. It may dry up completely or flood our sensations. We cannot close the book or turn off the switch. We can only flee.

The problem is compounded when we think of trying to share this kind of information with someone who is outside, who has not yet been taken in. But to clarify our plight let us draw a rather simple analogy. Supposing we have a friend we want someone else to meet. First of all, it would be meaningless to introduce a friend to people who are strangers to us too. That is the sort of travesty of the personal that occurs in political advertising. Both parties would have to be known in some direct way to us. We could not buy television time or newspaper space or rent a billboard and hope to accomplish the same thing that bringing them together in the same room would. We would draw upon their own attachment to ourselves to create an initial bond between them. We cannot, of course, guarantee the friendship. In fact, sometimes our very determination seems to defeat our ends. But it is the only way, unpredictable as it is, so far as I know, to share our knowledge of a person, whether human or divine, with another person.

If all this sounds simple-minded, that's because it is. The part of the brain that apprehends knowledge directly instead of abstractly has always been labelled primitive and childlike by our society. Yet we are so alienated from intimate knowledge and so enamored of anonymous, distancing information that here we have to take one step at a time, learning to walk like a child.

Individually and intimately we know Christ. We are for the most part quite inarticulate about this knowledge. But that is nothing to castigate ourselves for. We suspect the sincerity of those too glib about their love life. Yet by some crazy leap into frustration, we have been convinced that this knowledge of which we are unable to speak even to our neighbors can be transmitted whole and intact to strangers by two-dimensional bits of bluish-white light and disembodied voices.

It really is a very simple and obvious proposition I make: a person, whether human or divine, cannot be known—as a person rather than an image—except by immediate presence. If we want to project an image, either of Christians or the church, we can do that by means of television, magazines, books, billboards, movies, bumper stickers, buttons, records, and posters. If we want people to know Christ, we must be there face to face, bearing Christ within us.

And therein lies the great danger. A rejection of Christ becomes a rejection of ourselves, individually and painfully. Perhaps this is why we do not want to take the risk and why we are so eager to pile up a barricade of media technology between us and the unpredictable outside world.

Chapter VII:

SANCTUARY

"Step softly, under snow or rain,
To find the place where men can pray;
The way is all so very plain
That we may lose the way."—G. K. Chesterton

I HAVE MADE MY plea for a return to the bald and frightening facts of the inescapably intimate nature of evangelism which is necessarily in conflict with the overpowering anonymity of mass media. Every Christian must come to know God as Person, a knowledge that precludes disembodiment, distance, and superficiality. One must end up at last in Jerusalem in the Presence or go on forever aimlessly wandering the byways. Because the City of God is our destination it can transcend all the merely cultural paraphernalia of any man-made metropolis. It outlasts the Roman Empire, the medieval age of faith, the Renaissance, the Enlightenment, the westward migration, several world wars, the industrialization of work, and the Technological Society. It stands, fresh and gleaming, though difficult to discern, even amid the culture we now find at once so awesomely powerful and so woefully inadequate.

But having made my plea for a rejection of deceptive methods of spreading Good News, I would now like to wander down a path of particular interest to me. It is sometimes called culture and sometimes called art, a seeming distinction that will be dealt with later. It is the same road, however, and one that can lead either into or out of Jerusalem, to use C. S. Lewis's phrase. As such it is of secondary importance to the conclusions already reached in the last chapter. "Mere" Christianity always supersedes any of the means used to arrive at it. Yet all roads into Jerusalem should be kept in good repair and free of the sort of debris that can block the path of a pilgrim.

There have been those, for example, who have sought
to make this path of culture itself the ultimate destination
of mankind. Matthew Arnold for one proclaimed himself
"above all, a believer in culture" ("Culture and Anarchy,"
from *The Portable Matthew Arnold*, Viking, 1949, p. 471).
Of course he tried to mitigate his heresy by defining culture
as the "study of perfection." Still, he smacks, despite his
constitutional melancholy, of that nineteenth-century optimism that expected to find universal salvation in human
creations. Arnold believed he had escaped the self-deception
of his age by placing his bets on culture rather than phi-
listine industrialism. But today, looking back at his false
hopes through the intervening horrors of war and massive
atrocities, we are unconvinced and even embarrassed by his
naiveté: "It is in making endless additions to itself, in the
endless expansion of its powers, in endless growth in wisdom and beauty, that the spirit of the human race finds its
ideal. To reach this ideal, culture is the indispensable aid,
and that is the true value of culture" (p. 476). The human
race has indeed made seemingly endless additions to itself,
sought endless expansion and endless growth, but not often
in the direction of wisdom and beauty. The study of perfection, the sturdiest empiricist would concede, cannot successfully be made by unaided human capacities.

George Santayana in the next generation followed Arnold farther along this road out of Jerusalem that sought
salvation in culture. No longer does he speak of the study
of perfection, however. He claims instead to approach aesthetics through "naturalistic psychology," meaning that
studies in perfection are for him now reduced to a certain
stimulation of the senses (*The Sense of Beauty*, Scribner's,
1896, v). Preference is ultimately irrational. "Science is the
response to the demand for information," he says. "Art is
the response to the demand for entertainment" (p. 15). Our
whole structure of contemporary culture seems to be built
on those two premises. Even though Santayana comes only
a generation after Arnold, such cynical sophistication would
have been shocking to the author of "Sweetness and Light."

Yet Santayana's unalloyed secular reasoning is a direct result of misplaced faith "above all" in culture.

In fact, Santayana strikes us as offering a more honest
picture of what secular man can realistically hope for. "The
sad business of life is rather to escape certain dreadful evils
to which our nature exposes us,—death, hunger, disease,
weariness, isolation, and contempt. . . . The appreciation of
beauty and its embodiment in the arts are activities which
belong to our holiday life, when we are redeemed for the
moment from the shadow of evil and the slavery of fear, and
are following the bent of our nature where it chooses to lead
us" (p. 17). This notion of human culture, degenerated from
Arnold's ethereal original, offers to substitute the merely
pleasant for ecstasy, information for truth, and entertainment for art. It offers an opiate to assuage the gaping wounds
of life. This is what culture in its "endless additions" has
actually come to. In being elevated to the level of divinity,
it has had its clay feet exposed. Santayana no longer expects
culture to save us, only to distract temporarily our attention
from the pain and darkness that surround us.

But before we summarily dismiss the whole category of
culture, even our own, as unimportant and disposable since
it is indeed transitory and less than ultimate, let us also
realize that *we* are not the ones to transcend culture. As
long as we are caught in the web of time and are not yet
freed into eternity, we must breathe the air, however pol-
luted, of human culture. It may be that in some future state
we will inhale the finer atmosphere of unconditional being,
but for the moment we both give and are given in marriage,
rear children, bury bodies, all under certain cultural con-
ditions. And we should in some ways be grateful for this.
Culture can graciously provide a structure that shelters us
from the chaos of sensory anarchy. If we had to make decisions about even basic human functions that were not already provided for us by a cultural context, we would never
make it out of bed in the morning. Indeed there would not
even be beds to get out of, for beds, whether tatami mats or
water balloons, are cultural creations. It is in fact when the
choices available to an individual seem to become more

random, undetermined, and chaotic—when there are truly unlimited possibilities—that we know a culture is disintegrating.

Cultures have disintegrated before, and, being finite and less than ultimate, will continue doing so. A house to shelter human beings is a good thing, though never so good as to last forever. It has long been a truism that our culture is decaying; it is on the downward slope of the curve. T. S. Eliot was already writing in 1940 that "the tendency of unlimited industrialism is to create bodies of men and women—of all classes—detached from tradition, alienated from religion and susceptible to mass suggestion: in other words a mob" (*Christianity and Culture*, Harcourt, Brace, p. 17). In fact, it is possible to reach a stage of no culture at all, a state where human community and human creation disappears. There is no guarantee that a mere assemblage of human bodies will result in human culture. A mob is not a human civilization. It is something subhuman. This does not necessarily mean that its components are physically living among the rubble like refugees, even though their spirits may be. Certainly the structures of human community are devastated by war as thoroughly as physical buildings. People can be brutalized by bombs and terror. But automatons, though well fed and comfortable, are less capable of culture than even refugees.

"Culture," Eliot says, "may even be described simply as that which makes life worth living. And it is what justifies other peoples and other generations in saying, when they comtemplate the remains and the influence of an extinct civilization, that it was *worth while* for that civilization to have existed" (p. 100).

Here it may be well to explain what sometimes appears to be an equivocation on the word "culture." Some writers, Arnold and Santayana among them, seem to use the word to mean the arts and philosophy, a sort of elitist's illusion of human activity that eliminates much of the day-to-day work of the world. To their mind, only a few people are capable of participating in culture. Eliot and later writers are using a seemingly broader definition of culture that

comes to us from the relatively recent discipline of anthropology. In this view, the entire population participates in
their culture. But remnants from the past which we so carefully preserve give us a clue to the interaction between these
two apparently divergent definitions of culture. However
mundane and ordinary these remnants were in their own
day, they are precisely what comes to be recognized as the
art of that period through the simple process of attrition.
An Indian weaving a basket for storing seed corn hundreds
of years ago had no idea her work would end up in a museum
some day or be copied as an example of design and crafts-
manship. The sorts of things bequeathed to us unwittingly
from former ages of mankind somehow remain worthy of
our contemplation. They tell us something significant about
their creator's struggle with the world. Everything from
tombs to clay pots, bridges to songs, paintings to palaces.
We end by calling all these legacies art, even when they
were not conceived of in that sense in their own time.

In our own time we have segregated "art," as we have
religion, from culture in a way unknown to human civilizations before the Renaissance. China alone, uncorrupted
by the West the way Russia was in the nineteenth century,
has succeeded in integrating both its new spiritual enterprise of Maoism and its derivative art into its total culture.
We may consider both the religion and the art inferior, but
the energy generated by such a "cultural revolution" has
been enormous, the only modern parallel we have to the
medieval age of faith. Having never lived in anything but
a secular society, we are baffled by the appearance of a truly
pious culture in our midst. This religion may not have the
strength to outlast for long its founder or its exposure to the
West. But at least it serves as an instructive contemporary
example of a true culture, something found only in its dying
stages in the underdeveloped nations of the rest of the world.

In China one's very clothing is a statement of faith, not
unlike that of the Amish. Westerners are unable to understand the spirit of cheerful sacrifice they find there because
they no longer believe in the spiritual as a motivating force.
Yet compare the current culture of China to that of pre-

Renaissance Europe. Then even paintings were done by anonymous artists who were merely workers in the same way that potters and gardeners were workers. Paintings were as much a part of the whole culture as dishes or vegetables were. Medieval altar triptyches, so carefully preserved over centuries, were then the equivalent of the wall posters of modern China. They were a part of everyday life, accessible to all.

But now we in the West have specialized buildings called museums to hold these works we isolate as art. "Why is it difficult," asks Walker Percy, "to see a painting in a museum but not if someone should take you by the hand and say, 'I have something to show you in my house,' and lead you through a passageway and upstairs into the attic and there show the painting to you?" (*The Message in the Bottle*, p. 5).

Culture is the shelter for what is human. It is the sustaining evidence that man is man. The traces it leaves behind we have in retrospect learned to call art. The only thing we really know about prehistoric man, says G. K. Chesterton in *The Everlasting Man*, is that he drew pictures. But art and religion have now been institutionalized, or rather incarcerated, and are not allowed to mingle in society. They no longer permeate society with their spiritual experiments. There is no space for them other than as socializing mechanisms. Churches are tolerated because they turn out "good citizens" who help to shore up society. As soon as they are perceived as a threat to the efficient operation of that society, however, they are forced back into the confines of their own bailiwick. The line dividing church and state today runs along the perimeter of the building lot. Artists, except as they contribute their wares to commercial enterprise, are tolerated even less. The museum is more a prison than even the church. Thus we live more and more in a cultureless society, human beings deprived of shelter from inhuman forces.

We are making false assumptions when we compare ourselves to the early Christians in conflict with the Roman Empire. That was a case of a declining culture with multiple pagan religions being permeated and replaced by a renewed spirituality. Thus it will not do for us simply to fall back on the previous pattern of Christian martyrdom by a hostile state. For one thing, no one cares enough to throw us to the lions anymore. Nor is it realistic to dream of transforming culture through Christian activity. We live in a time when there is precious little culture to transform. What we live in is technology. If we throw ourselves upon the machinery of our society, we will meet with the fate of Charlie Chaplin, not Polycarp. One does not transform a machine.

T. S. Eliot in "Notes Toward the Definition of Culture" warns against "two complementary errors. The one more widely held is that culture can be preserved, extended and developed in the absence of religion. . . . The other error is the belief that the preservation and maintenance of religion need not reckon with the preservation and maintenance of culture: a belief that may even lead to the rejection of the products of culture as frivolous obstructions to the spiritual life" (p. 102). In other words, religion requires both theology and anthropology. God does not save technological apparati but human beings. Culture at the least nurtures humanity and keeps it from total absorption into either the bestial on the one hand or the mechanical on the other.

It is probably easier to convert an aborigine than technological man simply because the former still exercises his facility for worship. He can still apprehend the transcendent dimensions of reality. Albert Schweitzer has described the process of conversion in the Ogowe tribe who came to the mission station containing his hospital. "There lives within him a dim suspicion that a correct view of what is truly good must be attainable as the result of reflection. In proportion as he becomes familiar with the higher moral ideas of the religion of Jesus, he finds utterance for something in himself that has hitherto been dumb and something that has been tightly bound up finds release" (*The Primeval Forest*, p. 116). How impoverished the Western heathen in comparison whose technology allows for no reflection or release.

Yet we have come to accept as inevitable the process whereby an "underdeveloped" country is technologized and simultaneously has its indigenous culture plowed under.

The two processes are almost synonymous. Missionaries have been blamed for putting muu-muus on South Sea islanders, but that was minuscule in its cultural impact compared to the capture of native textiles by polyester, a sheerly industrial and unintentionally destructive phenomenon.

We have been misled into casting our questions about the tensions between culture and religion falsely. Christianity has always had difficulty in any period in history deciding upon its proper relation to the dominant culture it must inhabit. It has struggled to develop faithful modes of living in many worlds while not being of them. From ancient Roman pluralism to medieval monoliths to wandering dissenters, there is the fascinating orchestration of inward and outward, upward and downward movement. But now the terms have shifted entirely. We can no longer ask how religion relates to culture because we are rapidly approaching the point of no-culture. In culture's place we have only a society of sorts, the systems by which decisions are made about technology. Naturally, these decisions and systems affect all our lives. Building codes, market analyses, nuclear accords, safety standards. But they are not culture. Like polyester, they are not, cannot be, homemade.

Instead of culture today, we have life-style, a sop meant as a temporary appeasement of specifically human hungers. Life-styles attempt to simulate a culture, one that is rootless, ahistorical, and without tradition. One can wear the clothes of the 1930s, listen to the music of the 1950s, and eat Arab pita bread with Seventh Day Adventist alfalfa sprouts without ever knowing or caring about the soil that produced these accoutrements to life-style. Culture assumes there is something worth passing on to the next generation. This link between the past and present is called tradition, a word we are currently taught to despise. Life-style, however, assumes no continuity even within the same individual.

At a recent Cambridge Forum, "The Arts in the Year 2000," James Ackerman, a Harvard professor of fine arts, said, "We seem to have arrived at the first age in history that has no taste or style" (*Christian Science Monitor*, January 30, 1978, p. 12). This he attributes to the twin features of mass media and an "inherently homogenized" public. Although the melting pot ideal has been publicly replaced by the encouragement of ethnic minority pluralism, the fact is that these former bastions of culture do not stand a chance once they are exposed to mass media. Taco Bell, Kentucky Fried Chicken, Pizza Hut, Japanese Beef Bowl. Any fast-food strip in the country shows the effortless co-option of ethnic cultures.

The only culture we have, the only "taste or style," is pop culture, a self-consciously ironic synthetic culture. American pop culture is, quite literally, a joke. A cynical sneer whose intention is to insult its audience. Massive practical jokes, such as wrapping mountains in plastic, are contemporary artists' idea of creativity. "As a response to the abandonment of art by society," Professor Ackerman noted, "one artist even invited an audience to a locked gallery only to tell them that the work of art was the closing of the exhibition."

For one thing, our notion of beauty has been so called into question and undermined that everyone is a little embarrassed by the word now. It smacks of calendar art and a certain sort of softheadedness. What some theologians wanted to do with the word God has in fact been accomplished with the word Beauty. It has been stowed away as an artifact of a bygone era. Beauty is a word that has been bought out by Hallmark cards. There is either a total failure of nerve that degenerates into camp art and parody based on despair or else there is an austere, ethical approach whose aim is to sear the conscience of the age. The modern novel, for example, is an extended sermon filled with bleak illustrations of human depravity. The resulting guilt delights no one but the moral sadist, however, and in the end itself leads to despair. Susan Sontag, hovering between these two responses, shows clearly the contemporary terror of Beauty when she claims that any theory, "so far as it assumes that art is concerned with beauty, is not very interesting. (Modern aesthetics is crippled by its dependence upon this essentially vacant concept.)" (*Styles of Radical Will*, p. 31).

Yet the same artistic theorists who deny the possibility

of beauty, continue to probe the limits of intelligence in art.
They dabble in chimpanzee paintings and computer poetry.
Their unformulated question is: At what point will the light
fail? There is a certain perversity in all this that we somehow sense but haven't been able to define clearly. In not
acknowledging the source of all light they cannot know they
are testing God, attempting to explore the limits of his creative power. They—and we—have a vague sense of pushing
at some mysterious limit. We as God-fearers have also a
sense of uneasiness, of the dangerous nature of their enterprise, as though they might at some point go too far and fall
over the edge of the world into an abyss of either light or
darkness that would be their undoing.

Much of modern artistic endeavor, not just the chimpanzee or computer fringes, seems to be a probing of these
limits, limits that are not even acknowledged. It is as though
a blind man were to deny that sight was a reality, even a
possibility, and by his denial to put himself in the gravest
danger because he cannot see the ditch and refuses to be
guided.

The artist's position is indeed next to impossible. Beauty
has been stripped away from our culture by technology because it serves no useful purpose. It is meant to achieve no
measurable good for humanity. Supposedly the modern world
promises the artist everything. There are no limits, moral
or material, set on his activity. Yet, as the Catholic scholar,
Jacques Maritain, pointed out, he finds himself left without
"even the bare means of subsistence. Founded on the two
unnatural principles of the *fecundity of money* and the *fi-
nality of the useful*, multiplying needs and servitude without
the possibility of there ever being a limit, . . . the system of
nothing but the earth is imprinting on human activity a
truly inhuman mode and a diabolical direction, for the final
end of all this frenzy is to prevent man from resembling
God" (*Art and Scholasticism*, Scribner's, 1930, pp. 36-37).

As if this were not enough for the artist to contend with,
there is the *appearance* of Beauty that technology keeps
alive as a sop to those who still maintain a lingering reverence for the concept. This substitute for Beauty Maritain

calls "sensual slush." We know it too well, particularly in Christian media. The scarcely noticeable Muzak in the background, the shoddy plushness of public buildings, the vague sentiment of greeting card verse accompanied by a misty photograph of a verdant hillside or a sunset. The verses and the pictures are, by the way, now matched by computers.

No wonder the ordinary mortal wanders, properly chastened, through the echoing expanses of museum and theater, feeling attacked, humiliated, mystified, or bored. He shrugs his shoulders as he leaves. What does he know anyway? Art is for experts, an inside joke he hasn't gotten the point of. At home he turns on the television with a sigh. And there we are again, back in the arena of pop culture, of bread and circuses.

What Eliot said is true. Culture cannot exist without religion. Without a transcendent vision, whether of Osiris, Nirvana, or the mystic rose, human creativity caves in and crumbles. It leaves behind no sign that life in that age was worth living. It is religion that is the larger category of which culture is a corollary and not the other way round as we have been taught to think. In fact, Eliot goes so far as to say that a culture is essentially "the incarnation of the religion of a people." Thus, "bishops are a part of English culture, and horses and dogs are a part of English religion." Or at least such was the case in 1940. Forty years later in America, we can only be concerned about a Christian lifestyle, one which lives parasitically off whatever is technologically mediated to the entire populace.

Here and there we find small pockets of peoples who have tried to resist the cultural drought, people who still wear funny clothes and drive buggies. They are living museum pieces which no one expects to survive another generation. Or we see the pathetic attempts among ethnic minorities to resurrect the relics of their cultural heritages. Yet there is as little hope in the revitalization of American Indian cultures without a corresponding belief in the guardian spirits that called them forth as there is that a cultural renaissance should break out in Iran based on the worship of Zoroaster rather than oil.

When people stop believing in their divinities, they stop believing in everything else as well, even their own abilities to create. Where there is no prospect of holiness, there can be no sanctification of life. Without such sanctification, no care is given to the making of things. Efficiency replaces efficacy. Beauty becomes an empty category. Feeling which is quick replaces learning which is slow. The dismantling of the human shelter we call culture is inexorably logical.

But that is only half the problem. The second error that Eliot points out—"the belief that the preservation and maintenance of religion need not reckon with the preservation and maintenance of culture"—is perhaps more relevant to Christians. We have been so frightened in recent years, and rightly so, by the specter of civil religion that we have been blind to this particular error. But the very term itself—*civil* religion—emphasizes its essential basis in political systems rather than in culture. Because of our fears of making religion a mere handmaiden to the dominant political structures, we, like everyone else, have abandoned the human shelter of culture, leaving it to deteriorate from lack of care. Although Christians, unlike secular aestheticians, may not have despaired of the reality of Beauty, they have relegated it either to eternity or to something called Nature, a place where human creation cannot intrude. We too are unwilling to do the hard work, await the long, time-wound process of human culture. We want, like everyone else, quick results. What congregation would be willing to wait a hundred, even ten years, for the craftsmanlike completion of its sanctuary?

Yet if culture, as inherently human activity, survives at all, it will be under the guardianship of religion. I believe that much of the success of invading Eastern religions in this country has been due to the opportunity for experiencing culture they offer to a generation that has lived essentially cultureless lives. Diet, dress, discipline—all geared to a human scale and connected to deeply rooted traditions. When the counterculture movement failed (primarily because there was no actual culture to counter and the participants had no true idea of culture themselves), many from its disillusioned ranks simply dropped themselves on the doorsteps of cultures that still had some vitality, orphans pleading for adoption by Buddhists, Hindus, Moslems.

We may consider this a false way, but what have we offered in its place? To say that Christ is greater than any cultural formation is not to say that all cultural formations are therefore unimportant. He is also greater than any human government, yet we still recognize the necessity, even at times the blessing of, having governments. Still we have acquiesced, even abetted, the stampede toward the standardization, which means sterilization, of culture. In the interest of administrative efficiency we have united denominations that represented diverse cultural heritages. Under such bureaucracies have been buried artifacts that might have sustained human spirits. For example, there used to be recognizable regional (and also denominational) styles of architecture. Now not only can you not tell what part of the country a building was made for, it is often not even identifiable as a church at all. At a time when there is unprecedented willingness among groups of Christian laity to cooperate in the loose, unaffected mutuality of faith, ecclesiastical bureaucracies have insisted on systematizing such trust, aiming at one Protestant body that would absorb and obliterate important traditions. Centralization has become a primary value; locality has been seen as a negative one.

Infinite creativity demands infinite diversity. Such are the attributes of God. No duplicates, whether of snowflakes or fingerprints, come from the hand of God. And we, bearing his image, should recognize ourselves as sub-creators, to use Tolkien's term, rather than standardizers. Our concept of creativity may at times seem to be in conflict with culture. We think of the individual artist as always in revolt against his culture, and in some ways this is true. A culture is the creation of an organism made up of an entire people. A "work of art" is done by an individual. Poems and paintings are not made by committees. The relationship is, however, symbiotic. Shakespeare's England provided him with the cultural creations of kings and peasants, without which there would have been no plays. He in turn added to the common language stock in such a way that we are still feeding off it today. Culture undoubtedly "limits" the individual; Shakespeare was limited to the notions of monarchy and yeomanry. Yet limitation is not the same thing as standardization. Even God, limited by certain requirements when making a human being, nevertheless makes each one unique. Strangely, our secular society which promises us, and especially artists, a life without limits, is the most standardized in human history.

If human culture and the works it requires is to survive, persist, and be maintained in this age, it will only be through religious remnants. They are the only ones who affirm their likeness to God in creativity. In technological society such activity is simply beside the point, expendable. Such a society has no vested interest in sustaining what is essentially human in its populace. Quite the contrary. It has an interest in making them more and more predictable, more and more mechanical. Culture organizes the life of the senses so that it can apprehend and make manifest the life of the spirit. To a society that recognizes no such life, culture is extraneous.

I certainly have no "program" to propose for the church's maintenance of culture. Culture, in any case, is unconscious, something that cannot be directly aimed at. Those relics of past civilizations we marvel at today, whether cave drawings of reindeer or tapestries of unicorns, were not conceived as monuments or museum pieces. Unself-conscious, intuitive response is culture's essential nature and why it can never be a part of a purposeful technological society whose operating mode is conscious planning and evaluating in the interest of efficiency. There can be no long-range planning for nurturing culture by the church, although there can perhaps be a conscious effort to avoid attending to its extermination.

What there can be, however, is space. And time. The two components of our lives that electronic media seek to eradicate in their demand for the unspecified "here" and the transient "now."

A black Episcopal bishop at the last Lambeth conference gently reproached its hurried functioning by invoking the efficacy of time and place in his being. "I am from Africa, your grace," he said, "and I take my time." He was not concerned to convince the conference that he was just like everyone else. Neither his time nor his place was interchangeable with anyone else's. Are we still capable of honoring that? If so, we are possibly the only segment of society that is. It is then we become more than a segment. It is then we transcend society.

The local church strikes our incredulous society, even its own national officials, as something hopelessly provincial and homemade. It is, but not hopelessly so. In fact, the hope for a great many things may lie precisely there. Local churches are notoriously slow, even languid. They get caught up in candles and Christmas pageants and what color to paint the kitchen. They do not, to the despair of ecclesiastical executives, take proper notice of world issues. (Local churches, on the other hand, are never seen by their managerial superstructures as meaningful units of the "world.") In other words, the local church is a stubborn culture-carrier. No other agency does that in our society. Not schools, not governments, least of all media. With due respect to the genius of McLuhan in first recognizing the power of media, a "global village" is a contradiction in terms. Cultures are not sustained globally but locally.

If anything at all survives from this civilization, any pictures, any music, any stories, any stitches in time—in short, any single sign that we found life a joy rather than a joke—it will be preserved and maintained by a people obstinate in their particularity, people resisting both efficiency and despair, people taking their time and knowing their earthly place. That place is not Jerusalem certainly. Its scraps of pictures and shards of pottery will ultimately have to be left behind for others to stumble across and wonder at. But let them wonder at signs of something human, which is to say signs of the longings, the hope, and the promise of redemption. Then will their own road lead more surely to Jerusalem.